MACBOO
2023 COMPLETE

The Complete Illustrated, Practical Guide with Tips and Tricks to Maximizing the 2023 Macbook Air Like a Pro

Harold C. Hillyer

Copyright © 2023 Harold C. Hillyer- All rights reserved.

No part of this publication may be reproduced, stored in a retrieval system or transmitted in any form or by any means, electronic, mechanical, photocopying, recording, and scanning without permission in writing by the author

Contents

Introduction

There are two MacBook Air models available from Apple, one measuring 13.6 inches and the other 15.3 inches. The current-generation MacBook Air lineup gained a second model for the first time since the 11-inch model was retired with the introduction of the 13-inch model in June 2022 and the 15-inch model in June 2023.

There is no need for people who prefer a larger screen to spend more money on the MacBook Pro series because the 13- and 15-inch alternatives in the MacBook Air lineup are acceptable for both those who seek portability and those who prefer larger screens. The M2 Apple silicon chip, which has been around since 2022, is present in both MacBook Air variants.

The MacBook Air received a redesign in 2022, which Apple carried over to the new 15-inch model. The tapered shape that the MacBook Air had been using for so long has been replaced with a new chassis. Instead, the redesigned MacBook Air models take on the MacBook Pro's consistent, flat shape.

The 13-inch MacBook Air weighs 2.7 pounds and measures 11.3mm thick, making it slightly thinner than the previous model. With dimensions of 11.97 inches wide by 8.46 inches high, it is almost the same size as the model from the previous generation.

The 15-inch MacBook Air is 3.3 pounds heavier and 11.5mm thicker than the 13-inch version. Its dimensions are 9.35 inches in height by 13.4 inches in width.

A 15.3-inch Liquid Retina Display and an upgraded 13.6-inch Liquid Retina Display, both of which support 1 billion colors and have 500 nits of brightness, are surrounded by thin black bezels on the 13-inch and 15-inch models, respectively.

The improved 1080p FaceTime HD camera on the MacBook Air is surrounded by more screen real estate thanks to a notch at the top of the display. For the 13-inch MacBook Air, Apple incorporated a built-in four-speaker sound system that supports broad stereo and spatial music, while the 15-inch variant features a six-speaker system. There is a three-microphone array in both variants.

The MacBook Air is available in Silver, Space Gray, Starlight, and Midnight, a new dark blue color that is nearly black. The MacBook Air still has a big Force Touch trackpad and a black keyboard with Touch ID.

On the MacBook Air, there are two USB-C ports, a MagSafe port for charging, and a 3.5mm headphone socket with high-impedance headphone compatibility.

When viewing movies or television, the MacBook Air's battery may last up to 18 hours, while web browsing can last up to 15 hours. With a 70W USB-C power adaptor that is optional, it offers fast charging.

The MacBook Air from Apple has a second-generation M2 chip, which replaces the first M1 chip. The M2 chip supports up to 24GB of memory and has an 8-core CPU and up to a 10-core GPU. The M2 provides improvements in performance and economy over the M1 thanks to its 18% faster CPU, 35% faster GPU, and 40% faster Neural Engine. Despite the fact that the 15-inch MacBook Air was released a year after the 13-inch variant, both models use the same M2 chip.

The starting price for the 13-inch MacBook Air with M2 chip is $1,099, and after the 15-inch model was introduced, Apple introduced a $100 price reduction. Starting at $1,299, the 15-inch MacBook Air is also available with higher-priced SSD and processor upgrades for both versions. The M1 MacBook Air is still available from Apple for $999.

Design

In 2022, Apple completely redesigned the MacBook Air, the first significant redesign of the range since 2010. In place of the MacBook Air's long-standing tapered chassis, the upgraded model has a flat, MacBook Pro-style body that is the same thickness from front to back.

For individuals wanting for a cheap device with a larger screen, Apple released a new 15.3-inch MacBook Air in 2023 that uses the same design but has a larger display. With the difference of the chassis and display size, the designs of the 13-inch and 15-inch MacBook Airs are similar.

The 13-inch MacBook Air is almost the same size overall as the one from the previous generation, but there are a few minor variations. Its thickness of 11.3mm is considerably less than the previous model's (16.1mm) thickest point. Its dimensions are 11.97 inches long by 8.46 inches deep, and its weight of 2.7 pounds is slightly less than that of the 2.8-pound model from the previous generation.

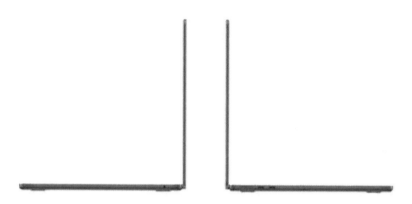

Of course, the 15-inch MacBook Air is bigger. It is somewhat thicker than the 13-inch version at 11.5 mm. It is larger, weighing 3.3 pounds, and measures 13.4 inches long by 9.35 inches deep.

Both devices have two Thunderbolt/USB-C connectors on their left sides, as well as a MagSafe charging port and a 3.5mm headphone jack. Another aesthetic feature borrowed from the MacBook Pro is the addition of four rubber feet by Apple.

Similar to the model from the previous generation, it has black bezels around the screen, a black Magic Keyboard without a Touch Bar, and a sizable Force Touch trackpad. It is simply a more compact and lightweight MacBook Pro.

In addition to Silver, the MacBook Air is also offered in Space Gray, Starlight (a light gold), and Midnight, a brand-new deep blue hue.

Trackpad and keyboard

The Magic Keyboard from the MacBook Air's predecessor is still in use. Unlike the butterfly keyboards that Apple utilized in earlier Macs, it has a scissor switch mechanism that can withstand dust and other contaminants without malfunctioning.

The keyboard on the MacBook Air has a scissor mechanism that provides 1mm of key travel, a steady key feel, and a rubber dome created by Apple that can store more potential energy for a key push that is more responsive. To illuminate the keys in dimly lit areas, the keyboard also has backlit keys that are controlled by an ambient light sensor.

The MacBook Air lacks a Touch Bar and includes a complete row of function keys, just like the M1 Pro and M1 Max MacBook Pro models.

A sizable Force Touch trackpad is located underneath the keyboard and is the same as in previous iterations.

Users of the Force Touch trackpad can press anywhere on the trackpad to receive the same reaction because it lacks conventional buttons and is powered by a collection of Force Sensors. Users receive tactile sensation when using the trackpad in place of the actual button press thanks to a taptic engine powered by magnets.

The Force Touch trackpad enables both a light push, which serves as a standard click, and a deeper press, or "force click," which functions as a different motion and, among other things, displays definitions for a highlighted word.

Touch ID

The Touch ID fingerprint sensor on the M2 MacBook Air is situated next to the function keys at the top of the keyboard. Your fingerprint data and private information are safe with Touch ID thanks to a Secure Enclave.

When a finger is placed on the sensor, Touch ID on the MacBook Air unlocks the computer without the need for a password. It may also be used to make Apple Pay transactions in Safari and takes the place of passwords for password-protected apps.

Ports The MacBook Air has a new MagSafe 3 charging port that is the same as the charging port added to the 14- and 16-inch MacBook Pro models. It also has two Thunderbolt 3/USB-C ports that offer transfer speeds of up to 40Gb/s.

MagSafe 3

Thunderbolt / USB 4

3.5 mm headphone jack

High-impedance headphones can be used with the 3.5mm headphone jack.

Display

The display size of the 2022 MacBook Air is 13.6 inches, whereas that of the 2023 MacBook Air is 15.3 inches. Each model has thin bezels and employs "Liquid Retina Display Technology." Similar to the MacBook Pro, the MacBook Air sports a notch to provide access to a 1080p webcam while providing additional display space.

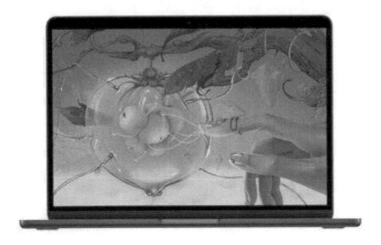

The resolution of the 13-inch MacBook Air is 2560 by 1664 with 224 pixels per inch, while the resolution of the 15-inch MacBook Air is 2880 by 1864 with 224 pixels per inch. Both screens feature P3 Wide color for vibrant, true-to-life colors and 1 billion colors. The maximum brightness is 500 nits.

The MacBook Air's display makes use of True Tone, a technology that adjusts color to better match ambient illumination. The MacBook Air models come with a multi-channel ambient light sensor that is used to power True Tone and can measure both the room's brightness and color temperature.

The MacBook Air can adapt the display's color and brightness to match the lighting in the room after determining the white balance, providing a more realistic viewing experience that also reduces eyestrain.

M2 Silicon Chip from Apple

Both the 13.6- and 15.3-inch MacBook Air models from Apple feature the M2 processor. The M2, which is the M1's successor, shares the M1's 8-core CPU but supports eight or 10 GPU cores, up from the M1's seven or eight.

Apple claims that the M2 processor has improved performance per watt and is constructed using cutting-edge 5-nanometer technology. It has 20 billion transistors, which is 25% more than the M1 and adds 100 GB/s of additional memory bandwidth.

The M2 chip outperforms the M1 by 1.4 times and the older MacBook Air models that were Intel-based by 15 times. It has a 40% faster Neural Engine, a 35 percent more potent GPU, and an 18 percent quicker CPU.

According to Geekbench benchmarks, the M2 chip performs multi-core operations up to 20% quicker than the M1 chip.

A single-core score of 1919 for the M2, which operates at 3.49GHz as opposed to 3.2GHz for the M1, is around 12% quicker than the 1707 single-core result for the M1 MacBook Air. The multi-core score for the M2 was 8928, up roughly 20% from the M1 model's score of 7419.

In terms of the Metal test, the M2 chip scored 30627, a significant increase from the M1 chip's score of 21001. The highest GPU core count of the M2 processor is 10, compared to the M1's 8 cores.

The M2 MacBook Air models can run quietly and without fans, just as the M1 MacBook Air.

Storage and Memory

Up to 2TB of SSD storage and 24GB of unified memory are supported by the M2 MacBook Air. The lowest models come with 256GB of storage and 8GB of memory.

Battery's life

A 52.6 watt-hour lithium-polymer battery powers the 13-inch MacBook Air, while a 66.5 watt-hour battery powers the 15-inch MacBook Air. Both devices last up to 18 hours when using the Apple TV program to view movies or up to 15 hours when wirelessly browsing the web, despite the greater battery in the 15-inch MacBook Air.

A 35W Dual USB-C Port Compact Power Adapter is included with the 13-inch MacBook Air with a 10-core GPU, whereas the standard model 13-inch MacBook Air comes with a 30W USB-C power adapter. Fast charging is made possible with a 70W USB-C power adapter that is an additional $20 option. Customers can choose the 70W USB-C power adapter for fast charging in place of the 35W Dual USB-C Power Adapter that comes with the base model 15-inch MacBook Air.

Connectivity

The WiFi standard 802.11ax, often known as Wi-Fi 6, is supported by the MacBook Air and is faster and more effective than 802.11ac WiFi. As well, Bluetooth 5.3 is supported.

Audio Devices and Microphone

The 13-inch MacBook Air has a four-speaker sound system with two tweeters and two ultrathin woofers for better stereo separation and vocal quality. The 15-inch MacBook Air has more room, so it has a six-speaker audio system with force-cancelling woofers for better sound. One of the minor distinctions between the 13- and 15-inch models is the sound system.

Wide stereo sound and spatial audio are supported by both MacBook Air speaker systems. When using the built-in speakers to play music or watch a movie with Dolby Atmos, spatial audio is accessible. Spatial Audio with dynamic head tracking is compatible with third-generation AirPods, AirPods Pro, and AirPods Max.

For improved sound clarity on video conversations, the MacBook Air also has a three-microphone array with directional beamforming.

FaceTime Camera The 2021 14- and 16-inch MacBook Pro versions include the same 1080p FaceTime HD camera as the MacBook Air. Apple claims it has twice the resolution and low-light capabilities of the previous generation and is driven by an improved image signal processor with computational video that enhances video quality.

Chapter 1

Set up your MacBook Air

When your MacBook Air starts up for the first time, Setup Assistant guides you through the straightforward procedures required to begin using your new Mac. You can opt to follow all the instructions or skip some and come back to them later. After initial setup, it could make sense, for instance, to set up Screen Time, which you can establish for various users.

The following is what Setup Assistant walks you through:

- **Choose your nation or region:** Your Mac's language and time zone are established when you do this.
- **Accessibility options:** Click Not Now to skip viewing accessibility options for people with vision, motor, hearing, and cognitive impairments.

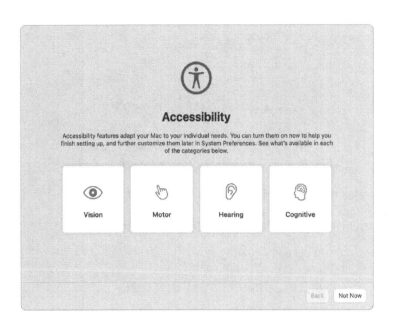

- **Join a Wi-Fi network:** Select the network and, if prompted, enter a password. You can also select Other Network Options if you're using Ethernet. To change the network at a later time, click the Wi-Fi status icon 📶 in the menu bar or click Wi-Fi in the sidebar of System Settings, then select a network and input the password. Here, you may also decide whether to turn on or off Wi-Fi.

  Advice: You can add the Wi-Fi status icon 📶 to the menu bar if you don't see it there after setup. Click Control Center in the sidebar of

System Settings, choose "Show in Menu Bar" under Wi-Fi, and then click OK.

- **Information transfer:** In the Migration Assistant window, select Not Now if you're setting up a new computer and haven't previously configured a Mac.

- **Log in with your Apple ID:** An email address and a password make up your Apple ID. It serves as your primary account for all transactions with Apple, including those involving the App Store, Apple TV app, Apple Books, iCloud, Messages, and other services. It's recommended to keep your Apple ID private and avoid sharing it. During setup, you can create an Apple ID for free if you don't already have one. Whether it's your PC, an iOS device, an iPadOS device, or an Apple Watch, sign in with the same Apple ID to utilize any Apple service.

You will see a panel for express setup, Make This Your New Mac, if you have already configured another device with macOS 12 or later, iOS 15 or later, or iPadOS 15 or later. Express setup uses the settings saved in your iCloud account and eliminates a lot of the stages.

- **Store your files in iCloud:** With iCloud, you can access your content—including documents, images, and more—from anywhere. Make sure to use the same Apple ID to log in across all of your devices. If you haven't already, visit System Settings and select "Sign in with your Apple ID" from the sidebar to set this option later. After logging in, pick the features you want to utilize by clicking iCloud, then clicking your Apple ID in the sidebar. During setup, you can also decide to use iCloud Keychain to store your credentials.

- **Screen Time:** Keep track of your computer use and get reports on it.

- **Enable Siri and "Hey Siri":** During setup, you can activate Siri and "Hey Siri" so that you can speak your Siri commands. Speak numerous Siri commands when prompted to activate "Hey Siri."

- **When configuring Touch ID:** you have the option of adding a fingerprint. Click Touch ID & Password in System Settings to set up Touch ID later or to add more fingerprints. Click $+$ and follow the on-screen directions to add a fingerprint.

On your MacBook Air, you may also choose how Touch ID should be used, including to auto-fill passwords, use Apple Pay, buy things from the App Store, Apple TV app, and websites, and unlock the computer.

Tip: Each user can add a fingerprint to Touch ID to rapidly unlock, authenticate, and log in to the MacBook Air if there are two or more users using the device. Each user account on your MacBook Air can have up to three additional fingerprints added to it, for a total of five fingerprints.

- **Configure Apple Pay:** During setup, you can configure Apple Pay for one user account on your MacBook Air. Other users are still able to use Apple Pay to make purchases, but they must do so with an Apple Watch or iPhone that has Apple Pay enabled. To add and verify your card, adhere to the onscreen instructions. You can be asked to verify a card if you've already used it to buy media.

Open System Settings and choose Wallet & Apple Pay to set up Apple Pay or subsequently add more cards. To set up Apple Pay, adhere to the onscreen instructions.

It should be noted that the card issuer decides whether your card can be used with Apple Pay and may require you to supply further information to finish the verification process. Apple Pay works with a wide variety of credit and debit cards.

- **Pick your style:** To change the appearance of your desktop, click Light, Dark, or Auto. Open System Settings, click Appearance, and then select a setting if you wish to change the one you selected during setup. Other appearance options are also available, including the size and color of sidebar icons and highlights.

Apple ID on Mac

You may access all Apple services with your Apple ID account. Use your Apple ID to access media in Apple Music, Apple Podcasts, Apple TV, and Apple Books, download apps from the App Store, keep your content current across devices with iCloud, create a Family Sharing group, and more.

Your Apple ID can be used to access more websites and apps.

Important: Not need to create a new Apple ID if you forget your password; simply click the "Forgot Apple ID or password?" button in the login window to get your password back.

Create Apple ID accounts for your children and use Family Sharing, which is covered in more detail later in this section, to share purchases and subscriptions if additional family members use Apple devices.

All in one location. Manage every aspect of your Apple ID from one location. Your Apple ID and Family Sharing settings are at the top of the sidebar in System Settings on your MacBook Air. If you haven't already, click "Sign in with your Apple ID" at the top of the sidebar to log in with your Apple ID.

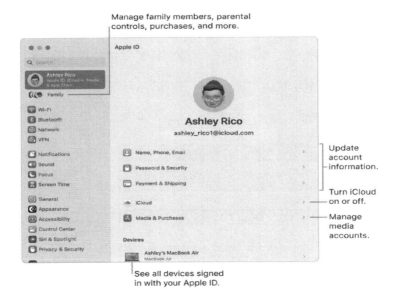

Manage family members, parental controls, purchases, and more.

Apple ID

Ashley Rico
ashley_rico1@icloud.com

Name, Phone, Email

Password & Security

Payment & Shipping

iCloud

Media & Purchases

Update account information.

Turn iCloud on or off.

Manage media accounts.

Devices

Ashley's MacBook Air
MacBook Air

See all devices signed in with your Apple ID.

Refresh your payment, security, and account information. Click your Apple ID in the sidebar of System Settings, then choose an item to review and amend the data related to your account.

- Overview: This section tells you if your account is set up and functioning properly; if not, it displays notifications and tips.
- Name, Phone, Email: Manage your Apple email newsletter subscriptions as well as the name and contact information connected to your Apple ID.
- Password & Security: Modify the password associated with your Apple ID, enable two-factor authentication, add or delete trusted phone numbers, and generate verification codes to sign

22

in to other devices or iCloud.com. You can control which websites and apps use Sign in with Apple.

- Payment & Shipping: Control the payment options connected to your Apple ID and the shipping address used for Apple Store transactions.
- iCloud: Click iCloud and then select the iCloud features you want to enable or disable. You can access any content on any device with iCloud turned on and signed in with the same Apple ID because when you enable an iCloud feature, your content is stored in iCloud rather than locally on your Mac.
- Media & Purchases: Choose your purchasing preferences and manage your subscriptions while managing the accounts connected to Apple Music, Apple Podcasts, Apple TV, and Apple Books.

View all of your gadgets. You can check the status of iCloud Backup for an iOS or iPadOS device, confirm that Find My [device] is enabled for each one, and remove a device from your account if you no longer own it from this list of all the devices connected to your Apple ID.

Using the family. You can create a family group with up to six members using Family Sharing. After that, you may share and control your purchases, share device positions, and flag lost devices in Find My. By setting screen time restrictions and creating Apple ID accounts for your children, you can control how your children use their devices. Click Family in System options to adjust your family sharing options.

Utilize Family Sharing to share purchases and storage. Even if they each have their own iCloud account, up to six members of your family can share the same storage plan and share purchases made from the App Store, Apple TV app, Apple Books, and iTunes Store. One credit card can be used for all family purchases, and your MacBook Air can be used to authorize purchases made by your children.

Account Restoration. To help you reset your password and restore access to your account, add one or more people you trust as recovery contacts or create a recovery key. Click Manage for Account Recovery after selecting Password & Security.

Heritage Contact. Select one or more people to serve as your Legacy Contacts so that they will have access to your account and personal data after your passing. Click Manage for Legacy Contact after selecting Password & Security.

Desktop, menu bar, and Help on your Mac

The desktop is the first thing you see when you turn on your MacBook Air. From here, you can open programs quickly, search the web and your MacBook Air, manage your files, and more.

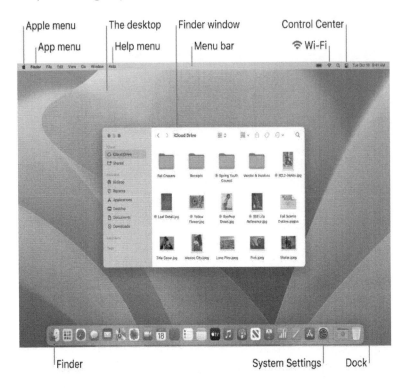

Apple menu · The desktop · Finder window · Control Center

App menu · Help menu · Menu bar · 📶 Wi-Fi

Finder · System Settings · Dock

Tip: Can't see the cursor on the screen? Move your finger quickly back and forth on the trackpad to briefly magnify it. Alternatively, move your mouse swiftly back and forth if you're using one.

Menu bar. The top of the screen is occupied by the menu bar. For app commands and task selection, use the menus on the left. Depending on the app you're using, the menu items change. To connect to a Wi-Fi network, check your Wi-Fi status 📶 , access Control

Center 🔘 , check your battery life 🔋 , use Spotlight

🔍 to search, and more, use the icons on the right

side of the screen.

Advice: The icons that display in the menu bar can be changed.

Apple menu . The Apple menu, which is always visible in the top-left corner of the screen, features frequently used items. Click the Apple icon to access it.

menu for the app. You can have several windows and applications open at once. To the right of the Apple menu , the name of the currently open app is displayed in bold, followed by the choices specific to that app. The name of the app menu and the menus in the menu bar change if you open a different app or click an open window in a different app, respectively. If you can't find a command in a menu, see if the desired program is running by browsing in the app menu.

Help menu. There is always support for your MacBook Air on the menu bar. To access the macOS User Guide, launch the Finder in the Dock, click the Help menu, and then select macOS Help. Alternately, enter a search term and select a suggestion. Open the app in question, then select support from the menu bar to access the support page.

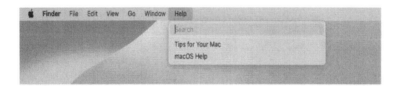

Maintain order with stacks. To keep your desktop tidy and keep your files grouped (by sort, date, or tag), you can stack them on the desktop. Place your pointer over a stack to see thumbnail images of the files inside it or click the stack to expand its contents to see what's inside. Click the desktop, then select View > Use Stacks to add stacks to it. Go to View > Group Stacks By and select an option to see grouping choices for your stacks. Then, whenever you add a new file to your desktop, it is automatically sorted into the appropriate stack.

Finder on your Mac

The Finder is the hub of your Mac, and it is symbolized by the blue icon with the happy face. Almost every file you have on your Mac, including documents, photographs, movies, and other files, may be organized and accessed using it. Click the Finder icon 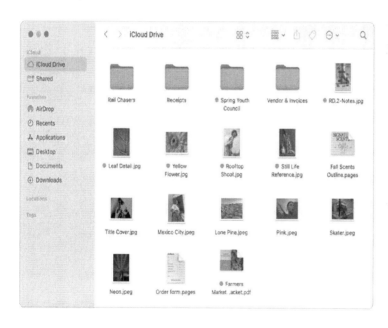 in the Dock at the bottom of the screen to launch a Finder window. To rapidly inspect a file's contents, force-click the file icon. To edit a file, force-click the filename.

Window of the Finder. To alter how you display files and folders, click the pop-up menu button at the top of the Finder window. View them in a list, a gallery, a hierarchy of columns, or as icons. The items you frequently use or want to open quickly are displayed in the sidebar on the left. Click the iCloud Drive folder in the sidebar to view every document you have on there. Click the Shared folder to only see the documents that have been shared with you and that you have been given access to. Select Finder > Settings to modify the sidebar's contents.

Be prepared. For typical sorts of information, including Documents, Pictures, Applications, Music, and more, folders have already been formed on your Mac. You can make new folders as you make documents, install applications, and complete other tasks to stay organized. Select File > New Folder to make a new folder.

Sync device. A connected device, such as an iPad or iPhone, shows up in the Finder sidebar. To access options for backing up, updating, syncing, and restoring your device, click its name.

Gallery View. You can identify your photographs, video clips, and other documents visually by using the Gallery View feature, which displays a sizable preview of the content you've chosen. You can identify the file you want by looking at the details in the Preview pane on the right. To find what you're looking for quickly, use the bottom scrubber bar. The Preview pane can be opened or closed by pressing Shift-Command-P. Select View > Show Preview in the Finder to display the options in the Preview pane. Select the settings for your file type under View > Show Preview settings to modify what is displayed.

Tip: To see filenames in Gallery View, press Command-J and choose "Show filename."

Gallery View

Preview Pane

Scrubber bar

Combine PDFs, trim audio and video files, and automate tasks.

Quick Responses. For shortcuts to manage and edit files directly in the Finder while in Gallery View, click the More button ⓘ in the bottom right corner of the Finder window. You can rotate photos, use Markup to annotate or crop them, combine images and PDFs into a single file, reduce audio and video files, use the Shortcuts app to launch shortcuts, and use Automator workflows to build custom actions (like watermarking files).

Look Quick. To launch Quick Look, choose a file and press the Space bar. To sign PDFs, cut audio and video files, annotate, rotate, and crop photographs without launching another software, use the buttons at the top of the Quick Look window.

Tip: Use Markup in Preview or Quick Look to create alternative image descriptions that VoiceOver can read.

Be there quicker. You may access folders and places quickly by using the Go menu in the menu bar. Go > Utilities is an alternative to utilizing multiple clicks to access the Utilities folder. To go back to the top level of nested folders, select Go > Enclosing Folder instead.

If you are aware of the location of a particular folder, select Go > Go to Folder, then type the location.

The Dock on your Mac

The programs and documents you use regularly can be kept in the Dock, which is located at the bottom of the screen.

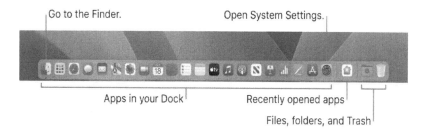

Go to the Finder.　　　　　Open System Settings.

Apps in your Dock　　　　Recently opened apps

Files, folders, and Trash

Start a program or file. To view all the apps on your Mac, click the Launchpad icon in the Dock or a specific app's icon in the Dock. Additionally, you may use Spotlight ⚲ (located in the menu bar's upper right corner) to search for an app and then launch it immediately from the search results. The central area of the Dock displays recently used apps.

Indicates an open app

Close the app. The window shuts but the application remains open when you click the red dot in the upper-left corner of an open window. A black dot appears beneath open programs in the Dock. Control-click the program icon in the Dock and select Quit to end the current app.

Put something on the Dock. You can move the object by dragging and dropping it. Files or folders should go in the right area of the Dock, and programs should go in the left.

Take something out of the dock. Drag the object from the Dock. The item is just removed from the Dock, not from your MacBook Air.

View every open file on your Mac. To open Mission Control, either press the Mission Control key on your keyboard or swipe with three fingers on your trackpad. View all of your open windows, desktop areas, full-screen applications, and more, and navigate between them with ease. The Mission Control icon can also be added to the Dock.

View every open window in a program. To see all of an app's open windows, force-click it in the Dock. Click once then press harder to force a click.

Tip: To modify the appearance and operation of the Dock, go to System Settings and select Desktop & Dock. You may alter the size of the Dock, relocate it to the left or right side of the screen, conceal it while not in use, and more.

Notification Center on your Mac

Your widgets, reminders, and other pertinent information are all conveniently stored in the notification center. Learn more about the events on your calendar, the financial market, the weather, and other topics, and review any notifications you may have missed (such as emails, texts, and other alerts).

Activate the Notification Center. Click the time or date in the upper right corner of the screen, or use two fingers to swipe left from the trackpad's right edge. See more by scrolling down.

Pay attention to what you're doing. Focus is able to automatically filter your notifications so you only see the ones you want to view when you're working, eating supper, or simply don't want to be interrupted. Focus can utilize a status in Messages to notify contacts that your notifications are hushed, and it can pause all notifications or only let certain of them to appear. Open System Settings, select Focus, and then select Add

Focus to configure Focus. Click⬮ in the menu bar, then select the Focus area and a Focus to switch on or off.

A Focus can be tailored to your current activities by allowing notifications from specific individuals or apps, for incoming calls or forthcoming events, among other things. Additionally, you can use Focus filters to block distracting items in apps like Calendar and Messages and share your Focus between devices.

Participate in your alerts. View event information, listen to the most recent podcast, or respond to an email. To examine options, take action, or obtain additional information, click the arrow in the top right corner of a notification.

Decide how you want to be notified. Select which notifications you want to see by opening System Settings, clicking Notifications. The most recent notifications are listed first.

Make your widgets unique. To add, remove, or reorder widgets, click Edit Widgets (at the bottom of your notifications). From the Mac App Store, you may also add widgets from other developers.

Control Center on your Mac

You can instantly access the features you use the most, like Bluetooth, AirDrop, Mic Mode, Screen Mirroring, Focus, brightness adjustments, and volume controls, from the menu bar thanks to Control Center, which collects all of your menu bar extras in one location. Open Control Center by clicking in the screen's upper-right corner.

For more possibilities, click. To view more possibilities, press a button. To view your favourite networks, other networks, or to access Wi-Fi Settings, for instance, click the Wi-Fi button . Click once more to return to the main Control Center display.

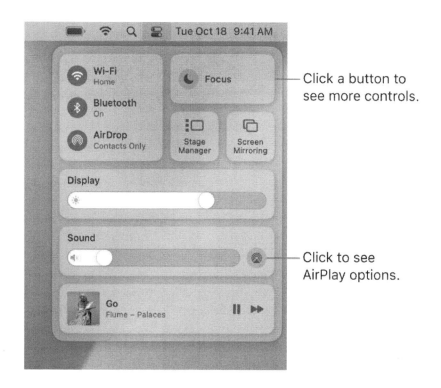

Click a button to see more controls.

Click to see AirPlay options.

Control the desktop. You can rapidly navigate between your apps and windows by using Stage Manager to group them together in one view. Additionally, you may combine apps to make workspaces that are perfect for your productivity.

Watch your microphone. The recording indicator lets you know whether or not your computer's microphone is currently in use. By alerting you whether an app has access to the microphone, this light improves security and privacy on your Mac.

Your Control Center favorites are pinned. You may instantly access a favorite item with just one click by dragging it from Control Center to the menu bar and pinning it there. You may see a preview of where the control will show in the menu bar by opening Control Center settings, then using the dropdown menu next to each module to select "Show in Menu Bar." There are several items that cannot be added to or removed from the menu bar or Control Center.

Tip: Press and hold the Command key while dragging an item out of the menu bar to rapidly delete it.

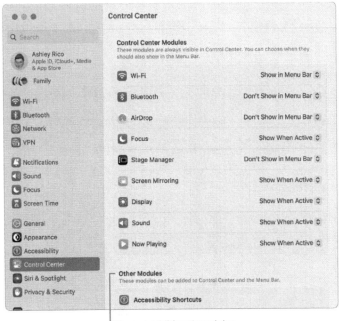

Choose additional modules to add to Control Center.

System Settings on your Mac

You may customize the settings on your MacBook Air in System Settings. For instance, you can modify your Mac's sleep settings using the Lock Screen. Alternatively, add a desktop background using the Wallpaper options.

Make your MacBook Air your own. To change a setting, click it in the sidebar of the System Settings sidebar, the System Settings icon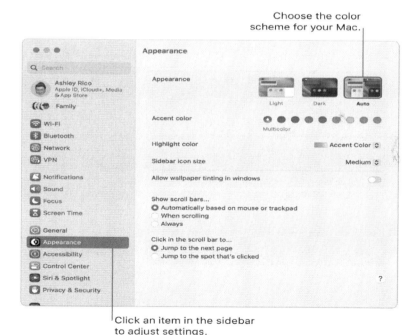 in the Dock, or Apple menu > System Settings. You might need to scroll down to see more settings.

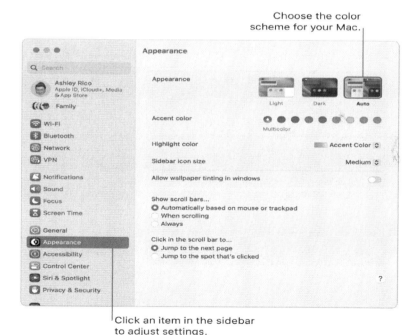

Choose the color scheme for your Mac.

Click an item in the sidebar to adjust settings.

Update macOS: Check to see if your Mac is running the most recent version of macOS by clicking Software Update under General in System Settings. Options for automated software upgrades are available.

Spotlight on your Mac

On your MacBook Air, Spotlight $\mathcal{Q}$ makes it simple to find anything, including photos, documents, contacts, calendar events, and email messages. Spotlight can also be used to launch apps or carry out short tasks like setting a timer.

Any topic can be searched. Start typing by clicking in the upper right corner of the screen. You can also use your keyboard's Spotlight $\mathcal{Q}$ key (F4). Spotlight can look for text in photos using Live Text. Not every language is offered.

Tip: To display or hide the Spotlight search field, press Command-Space.

Start typing, and results appear quickly.

Launch an app. Spotlight the app name, then press Return.

Take swift action. With Spotlight, you can complete some actions more quickly, such as creating a shortcut, initiating a Focus, or setting an alarm. Search for the action you wish to take after opening Spotlight. For instance, to start a timer from Spotlight, type Clock and then select Create Timer.

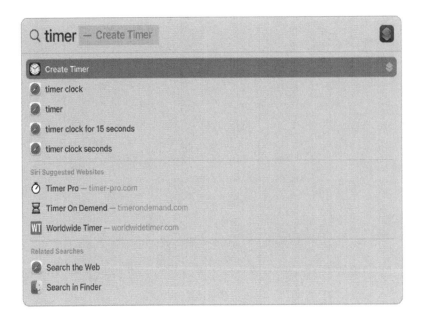

Convert measurements and currencies Type in a currency, such as $, €, or, and press Return to see a list of converted values. Alternatively, for conversions of measurements, indicate a unit of measurement.

Use Siri's recommendations. When you search with Spotlight, Siri Suggestions include information from Wikipedia articles, web search results, news, sports, weather, stocks, movies, and other sources.

Open System Settings, click Siri & Spotlight, and then click to deselect Siri Suggestions in the list of Search Results if you just want Spotlight to look for objects on your MacBook Air. The set of categories for Spotlight searches can also be altered.

Siri on your Mac

On your MacBook Air, you may activate Siri using your voice and use it for a variety of activities. You can, for instance, set up meetings, alter the settings, receive responses, send messages, make calls, and add events to your calendar. You can ask Siri questions like "How do I get home from here?" and "How high is Mount Whitney?" and use Siri to execute simple chores like "Create a new grocery list" and much more.

If the "Listen for 'Hey Siri'" option is turned on in Siri's settings, Siri will always be available when you say "Hey Siri" and will speak your request right away.

Reminder: Your Mac needs to be online in order to use Siri. Siri may not be accessible in all locales or in all languages, and functionality may differ depending on location.

Activate and enable Siri. Set preferences by clicking Siri & Spotlight in System Settings. If Siri was turned on during setup, hold down the Dictation/Siri (F5) key to bring up Siri. Alternately, turn on Ask Siri by clicking Siri & Spotlight in System Settings. Other Siri options include language and voice selection, as well as whether or not to display Siri in the menu bar.

Advice: By choosing that option in Control Center settings, you can add the Siri icon to the menu bar. To utilize Siri, simply click the Siri symbol.

Hello, Siri. Simply say "Hey Siri" on your MacBook Air to get answers to your inquiries. Click "Listen for 'Hey Siri'" in the Siri & Spotlight settings of System

Settings, then say a number of Siri instructions when prompted to enable this capability.

When the lid of your MacBook Air is closed, "Hey Siri" doesn't answer for your convenience. You can still call Siri from the icon in the menu bar even if the lid is closed and linked to an external display.

Turn on some music. Say "Play some music," and Siri will take care of the rest. Even Siri may be instructed to "Play the top song from March 1991."

Drop and drag. Drag & drop images and locations into an email, text message, or document from the Siri window. Text can also be copied and pasted.

Modify your voice. Select a selection from the Siri Voice menu by clicking Siri & Spotlight in the System Settings window.

You'll discover ideas for using Siri throughout this manual; they look like this:

Dial Siri. Use a phrase like:

- "Show me my reminders."
- How old is it in Paris?"

Window management on your Mac

It's simple to end up having a dozen open apps on your desktop, each with one or more windows open. Fortunately, there are a few effective ways to view and use the windows that you have open. You can enlarge one app to take up the entire screen when you need to concentrate, or you can select two apps to share the screen. Utilize Stage Manager to automatically arrange your apps and windows so you can easily switch between tasks and maintain a clutter-free desktop. Use Mission Control to display all of your open windows in a single layer so you can quickly locate a window that has been hidden. You can spread out your work across several desktops using numerous desktop spaces, making it simple to switch between them.

Click to see
window options.

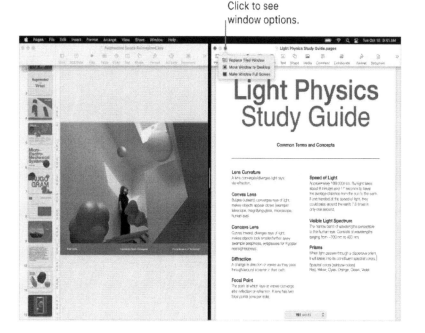

Utilize the entire screen. When you want your program to take up the entire screen, use full-screen mode. Keynote, Numbers, and Pages are just a few of the Mac apps that enable full-screen viewing. If you select to always show the menu bar, it will not be seen in full screen mode until you move the pointer over the top of the screen. Move the mouse pointer over the green button in the top-left corner of the window, then select Enter Full Screen from the menu that appears, to enter or exit full-screen mode.

Divvy up the screen. To work in two program windows simultaneously, use Split View. The two windows fill the screen like full screen. Choose Tile Window to Left of Screen or Tile Window to Right of Screen from the menu that displays by moving the pointer over the green button in the upper-left corner of the window you wish to use. When you select another window, the other half of the screen is instantly filled with it. The menu that shows when the pointer is over the green button includes choices to move between apps, make the two windows full-screen, and more.

The stage manager. Automatically arrange your windows and programs to keep your desktop clean. Your other windows are grouped on the side and are easily accessible with a single click, leaving the area you want to concentrate on front and center. Click Stage Manager in Control Center once it's open.

Mission Management. Move all of your open windows into a single layer quickly, then click a window to switch back to standard view with that window active in the foreground. A row of your split-view apps or additional desktops (spaces) will show up at the top of the screen. Press ⬒⬓ the top row of your keyboard or the Control-Up Arrow key to enter or exit Mission Control. The Mission Control icon ▦ can also be added to the Dock.

when just one desktop won't do. Create different desktop locations for your app windows and switch between them while you work. Enter Mission Control and select the Add Desktop button to create a place. To navigate between your spaces, use Mission Control and the keyboard shortcuts. As you work, you can add or remove gaps and drag windows from one place to another.

That horizontal traffic signal. The top-left corner buttons in each window are red, yellow, and green, and they have a purpose. To close an application window, click the red button. This ends the app's current session and closes all open windows for some apps. Others see the current window closed while the app remains open. The yellow button momentarily shuts the window and docks it on the right side. Click it in the Dock to enlarge it when you wish to reopen it. Additionally, you may quickly switch your windows to full screen, Split View, and more by using the green button.

Display settings for your Mac

Adapt your lighting to the environment. True Tone technology is present in your MacBook Air. For a more natural viewing experience, True Tone automatically adjusts the color of the display to match the light in your surroundings. In the Displays section of System Settings, turn True Tone on or off.

Utilize a flexible desktop. When you use a dynamic desktop image, the desktop image dynamically adjusts to reflect the local time. In System Settings, select Wallpaper, then pick a picture for Dynamic Desktop. Enable Location Services to have your screen adjust according on your time zone. The image adjusts according to the time zone provided in the Date & Time settings if Location Services are disabled.

Use Dark Mode to maintain your focus. The desktop, menu bar, Dock, and all other built-in macOS applications can all be made to utilize a dark color scheme. While controls and windows are dimmed, your content pops out in the foreground and takes center stage. In apps like Mail, Contacts, Calendar, and Messages, you can see white text on a black background to make it easier on your eyes when working in dimly lit areas.

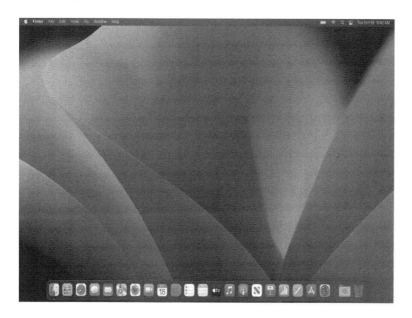

Colors and minute details stand out against the dark app backgrounds in Dark Mode, which is specifically designed for professionals who edit photos and images. However, it's also fantastic for anyone who wants to just concentrate on their content.

Night shift. To lessen your exposure to harsh blue light, set your Mac to warmer hues at night or in low light situations. Warmer screen colors may make it easier for you to fall asleep because blue light can make it difficult to do so. Night Shift can be set to automatically turn on and off at predetermined intervals, or to operate from dusk until dawn. Set your preferences by selecting Displays, clicking the Night Shift icon at the bottom, and then clicking System Settings. To change the color temperature, move the slider.

Connect a display. Your Mac can be connected to an HDTV, a projector, or an external display.

Transfer your data to your new MacBook Air

It's simple to wirelessly transfer your files and settings to your MacBook Air from another Mac or PC. From an existing computer or a Time Machine backup on a USB storage device, you can transfer data to your MacBook Air.

Migration Assistant requires macOS 10.7 or later, so you may need to upgrade your older machine's macOS version before you can transfer the data on it. However, it's advisable to update your older computer to the most recent version available.

Tip: Make sure your new MacBook Air is running the most recent version of macOS for optimal results. To check for updates, open System Settings and select General > Software Update.

Switch to a Mac from a PC. See Transfer info from a PC to Mac in the macOS User Guide if you're new to Mac and want to transfer data from a Windows computer.

Transfer wirelessly. You can utilize Migration Assistant whenever you want if you didn't move your data when you first set up your MacBook Air. Open a Finder window, navigate to Applications, choose the Utilities folder, double-click Migration Assistant, and then adhere to the prompts on the screen. Keep the computers close to one another throughout the migration process, and make sure they are both linked to the same network.

Tip: Ensure that both of your computers are linked to the same network in order to wirelessly transfer data from your current computer to your MacBook Air. Throughout the migration procedure, keep the two computers close to one another.

You can copy the files from the storage device to your MacBook Air if you used Time Machine to back up your data from another Mac to a storage device (such an external disk).

From a storage device, copy files. If required, attach the storage device to your MacBook Air using the proper adaptor. Then drag files to your MacBook Air from the storage device.

Back up and restore your Mac

It's crucial to frequently back up your MacBook Air in order to keep your files secure. Using Time Machine, which is a feature of your Mac, to back up your programs, accounts, settings, music, photographs, videos, and documents is the simplest method of backup. The macOS operating system is not backed up by Time Machine. To back up data to a compatible network volume or an external storage device linked to your MacBook Air, use Time Machine.

Get Time Machine ready. Ensure that your MacBook Air and the external storage device are connected to the same Wi-Fi network, or connect the external storage device to your MacBook Air. Open System Settings, select Time Machine under General, and then select Add Backup Disk. You're ready to go once you choose the drive you want to use for backup.

Utilize iCloud to backup. Time Machine backups do not need to include files in iCloud Drive and photographs in iCloud photographs because they are automatically stored in iCloud. However, if you want to support them, take the following actions:

- To disable Optimize Mac Storage for iCloud Drive, open System Settings, click Apple ID, then click iCloud. Your backup will be kept on your Mac and will contain the data in your iCloud Drive.
- iCloud Photos: Open Photos, pick Photos > Settings, then click iCloud and choose "Download Originals to this Mac." Full-resolution copies of your entire photo library will be kept on your Mac and added to your backup.

Restore your files. You can restore all of your files at once with Time Machine. If the Time Machine icon isn't in the menu bar, choose Apple Menu > System Settings, click Control Center in the sidebar, then click the pop-up menu next to Time Machine on the right, then select an option. Select one or more items that you want to restore (individual folders or your entire disk), then click Restore.

You can restore your files if the operating system or startup drive on your Mac is destroyed if you use Time Machine to backup your computer. Before you can recover your files from your Time Machine backup, you must first reinstall macOS on your Mac.

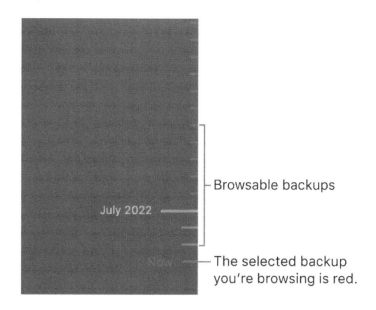

July 2022

Browsable backups

The selected backup
you're browsing is red.

Reinstall macOS: Your operating system files are kept apart from your personal files in a sealed system disk, therefore you should reinstall macOS. However, some acts, including as wiping out data or unintentionally harming a disk, need restoring your MacBook Air. You can use Time Machine to recover your personal files from your backup after reinstalling macOS. You can recover your Mac in a few different ways with macOS Big Sur and later. Installing a newer version of macOS than what came with your computer or what you were running before the disk was damaged may be necessary.

Important: To reinstall macOS in the future, advanced users may want to construct a bootable installer. If you want to use a particular macOS version, this may be helpful.

Restore factory defaults. Erase your Mac, then use macOS Recovery to reinstall macOS to return it to its initial configuration.

Accessibility on your Mac

Powerful tools are built into your Mac, iOS devices, and iPadOS devices to make Apple product features accessible and simple to use for everyone. For your Mac, there are four key accessibility emphasis areas.

- Vision
- Hearing
- Mobility
- Cognitive

Visit Accessibility for thorough information regarding accessibility assistance in Apple devices.

settings for accessibility. It is easier to locate what you're looking for in System Settings because the accessibility settings are categorized by the senses of vision, hearing, and motor.

(Beta) Live captions. Conversations, audio, and video can all have real-time subtitles added. Not accessible in all locales, nations, or languages.

Use voice control for everything. Your voice alone can be used to operate your Mac. Your Mac handles all audio processing for Voice Control, keeping your sensitive information safe.

precise dictation. If you can't manually type, good dictation is necessary for communicating. The most recent developments in machine learning for speech-to-text transcription are brought by Voice Control.

Spell out personalized words letter by letter. To assist Voice Control understand the terms you frequently use, you can also add custom words. Select Vocabulary under Voice Control in System Settings > Accessibility, then enter the desired words. Choose to maintain the preset commands or add new ones by clicking Commands on the Voice Control settings page.

English (US, UK, India, Australia), Mandarin Chinese (Mainland China), Cantonese (Hong Kong), Japanese (Japan), Spanish (Mexico, Latin America, Spain),

French (France), and German (Germany) are the languages for which dictation accuracy has improved.

Editing of rich text. With the use of Voice Control's rich text editing capabilities, you may make adjustments right away and continue speaking your next thought. You may precisely select text, quickly move the pointer to make modifications, and replace one phrase with another. Word and emoji recommendations let you rapidly choose what you want when you correct text. One example is "Replace 'John will be there soon' with 'John just arrived'."

A thorough navigation. To open and use apps, use voice commands. Simply pronounce an item's accessibility label name to choose it. Additionally, if you want to see number labels next to all of the clickable items, you can say "show numbers" and then speak a number to click. Say "show grid" to overlay a grid on your screen and perform actions like clicking, zooming, dragging, and more if you need to touch a portion of the screen without a control.

Zoom and hover. To show high-resolution text for screen elements behind your pointer, use hover text. When the pointer is over text and Command is pressed, a window with zoomed text displays on your screen.

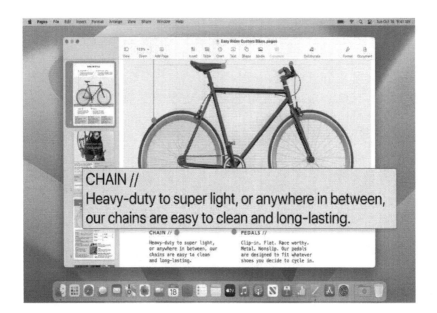

You can keep one monitor closely zoomed in while using the usual resolution of the other with Zoom Display. View the same screen from a distance and up close at the same time.

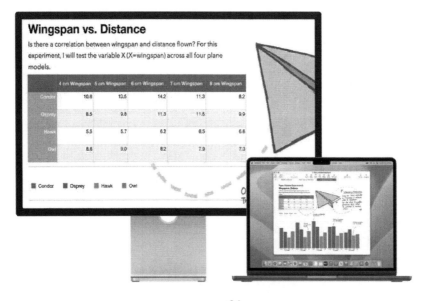

Create an intuitive custom pointer. You can alter the mouse pointer's contour and fill color to make it simpler to see when it moves or transforms into an insertion point, crosshair, hand, or other object.

Improved access to a keyboard. You can operate every aspect of your Mac with a keyboard alone, without the assistance of a mouse or touchpad, thanks to an enhanced range of keyboard shortcuts.

Use the built-in screen reader, VoiceOver. VoiceOver speaks the text in documents, webpages, and windows while reading aloud what is displayed on the screen. You can use VoiceOver to manage your Mac by using the keyboard or trackpad, or you can use it in conjunction with a refreshable braille display. Use the VoiceOver Utility to modify VoiceOver.

Dial Siri. Use a phrase like:

- "Enable VoiceOver."
- "Disable VoiceOver."

To use VoiceOver, use Siri. You can utilize Siri for VoiceOver or Speech if you like her voice more naturally. VoiceOver navigation is made even easier thanks to simplified keyboard navigation, which involves less digging into certain focus groups. Additionally, you can select from the International Braille tables and store your own punctuation marks in iCloud. In the Xcode text editor, VoiceOver now calls out line numbers, break points, warnings, and errors for developers.

Voice-over descriptions of images. You can add alternate image captions that VoiceOver can read by using Markup in Preview or Quick Look. Numerous approved apps for the iPhone, iPad, and Mac can read image captions, which survive sharing.

VoiceOver descriptions of PDF signatures. Your PDF signatures should include personalized descriptions so you can immediately recognize them and select the appropriate one.

Improvements to color. You can modify the colors on your Mac display if you suffer from a color vision impairment by using a different color filter. By touching Touch ID three times, you may open the Accessibility Options panel, where you can rapidly toggle this setting on or off to quickly distinguish a color.

Background sounds. With relaxing sounds like the ocean or rain, undesired environmental noise can be muted and distractions are reduced.

Customize your Memoji. Your Memoji should also include oxygen tubes, cochlear implants, and a soft helmet for headgear.

Chapter 2

Use your MacBook Air with iCloud and Continuity

You may collaborate with loved ones and keep your information current across all of your devices using iCloud. When you use iCloud and sign into each device with the same Apple ID, your MacBook Air works seamlessly with your iPhone, iPad, iPod touch, or Apple Watch. You can transfer files, share and edit documents, use your iPhone's camera as a webcam for your MacBook Air, switch between tasks, and more.

Open System Settings, choose "Sign in with your Apple ID" in the sidebar, and sign in using your Apple ID—or establish a new Apple ID if you don't already have one—if you didn't enable iCloud when you first configured your Mac. Toggle iCloud features on or off after clicking iCloud after signing in.

Use various devices to access your content. You can safely store, edit, and share your documents, photographs, and videos with iCloud across many devices to stay current.

Make use of additional devices with your MacBook Air. Utilize Continuity to transfer content between your MacBook Air and other devices without any hassle. When your MacBook Air and devices are close to one another, all you have to do is sign in on each one using your Apple ID for seamless collaboration. You may copy and paste information between devices, use your iPhone as a webcam for your MacBook Air, start a task on one device and finish it on another, make calls or send messages from your MacBook Air, and more.

Access your iCloud content on your Mac

Your most crucial data, including files, images, and more, is kept safe, current, and accessible across all of your devices with the aid of iCloud. Every Apple gadget has it built in, and everyone starts with 5 GB of storage. Your available space is not affected by purchases you make from the iTunes Store, Apple Books, Apple TV app, or App Store. If you have an iPhone, iPad, or iPod touch, all you need to do is sign in with your Apple ID on each device, turn on iCloud, and you're good to go. If you require more storage and premium services like iCloud Private Relay, Hide My Email, Custom Email Domain, and HomeKit Secure Video compatibility, you can subscribe to iCloud+.

iCloud Drive will automatically store your desktop and Documents folder. You can save files to your desktop or Documents folder, and they will be automatically made available on iCloud Drive so that you can view them from anywhere. You can access files on your MacBook Air, your iPhone or iPad in the Files app, the web at iCloud.com, or a Windows PC in the iCloud for Windows app when using iCloud Drive. Anywhere you access the file, your adjustments will be visible when you make changes to it on a device or in iCloud Drive.

To activate iCloud Drive, enter System Settings, select your Apple ID from the sidebar, click iCloud, and then select On.

Share and save pictures. Store your photo library in iCloud to access your pictures, movies, and modifications across all of your devices. Open System Settings, select your Apple ID from the sidebar, select iCloud, and then toggle Photos on to begin using iCloud Photos.

To share pictures and videos with up to five additional people, use iCloud Shared Photo Library. Everyone has the ability to modify the shared library, including adding new content, editing existing content, and adding comments. Smart suggestions make it simple to add certain photos from your collection, including pictures of a particular person or ones that were taken on a particular date. Go to Photos > Settings, select the Shared Library tab, and then follow the on-screen directions to get started.

Anywhere, enjoy your shopping. No matter which computer or device you used to make the purchase, your purchases from the iTunes Store, Apple Books, Apple TV app, and App Store are always accessible when all of your devices are signed in with the same Apple ID. So you can access all of your books, movies, music, and other media wherever you go.

Utilize Find My Mac to find your MacBook Air. If you have Find My Mac activated and your MacBook Air disappears, you may use it to locate it on a map, lock its screen, and even remotely erase its data. Open System Settings, select iCloud from the sidebar, then click your Apple ID to activate Find My Mac.

Please take note that only one user account on your MacBook Air may have Find My Mac enabled.

Make more using iCloud+. You may get all of the storage levels and sharing options of iCloud with the subscription service iCloud+, along with extra capabilities. Through Family Sharing, you can share any iCloud+ storage plan size. Additionally, iCloud+ comes with HomeKit Secure Video, iCloud Private Relay, and personalized email domains for your iCloud.com Mail account. What you receive from an iCloud+ subscription is as follows:

- Storage: iCloud storage options of 50 GB, 200 GB, or 2 TB.

- iCloud Private Relay: Private Relay is a service that safeguards your unencrypted communication and masks your IP address in Safari. You can browse the web more privately and securely when it is turned on.

- Hide My Email: You can send and receive email without disclosing your personal email address by creating one-of-a-kind, arbitrary email addresses that forward to your inbox.

- Connect your home security cameras in the Home App to record footage and access it from anywhere. All of the video is end-to-end encrypted, and none of it uses up any of your iCloud storage.

- Custom email domains: Add a unique domain name to your iCloud Mail address. Your family members' iCloud Mail accounts might be invited to use the same domain.

- Family Sharing: Each iCloud+ plan may be shared with up to five family members, allowing everyone to take use of the included storage and features with just one subscription.

Screen Time on Mac

You can keep an eye on what your children are doing on their Apple devices by using Screen Time, which also provides capabilities to make it simple to leave your MacBook Air when you need to take a break.

Examine your MacBook Air usage. View reports to find out which apps notify you the most, how much time you spend using apps and websites in a day or a week, and how frequently you pick up your device each day. Click App Usage, Notifications, or Pickups after opening System Settings and selecting Screen Time from the sidebar.

Establish boundaries. Set time restrictions to manage how much time you spend using particular apps, app categories, and websites. Select Downtime under Screen Time, then design a weekly program or a daily schedule for each day of the week.

Control your children's screen time. On their Mac, iPhone, or iPad, parents may establish Screen Time, and everything is configured for their children's devices. For the Music and Books apps, you may also establish media age ratings.

Don't overlook the crucial details. Decide which websites or apps you must always have access to. Select Always Allowed under Screen Time, then enable any apps you wish to have access to during downtime.

Use Handoff on your Mac

With Handoff, you may pick up where you left off on one device on another. When you return to your workstation, transfer the FaceTime call from your iPhone to your MacBook Air. Alternatively, start a presentation on your MacBook Air and continue it on your iPad. Messages can be viewed on an Apple Watch and replied to on a MacBook Air. FaceTime, Safari, Mail, Calendar, Contacts, Maps, Messages, Notes, Reminders, Keynote, Numbers, and Pages are all compatible with Handoff.

You must have an iPhone, iPod touch, or iPad with iOS 8 or later installed in order to utilize Handoff. Make that the Wi-Fi and Bluetooth are turned on and that you are logged in with the same Apple ID on your MacBook Air, iOS device, or iPadOS device.

Switching between devices. When your MacBook Air and other devices are close to one another and the activity may be transferred between them, an icon will often display in the Dock; click the symbol to transfer the activity between your devices.

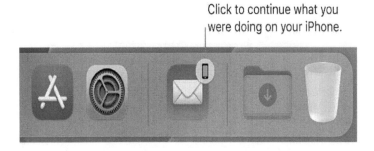

Click to continue what you were doing on your iPhone.

There is no handoff symbol for FaceTime in the Dock. Instead, click ⬜️Switch in the menu bar of your Mac, then click Join in the FaceTime window if you wish to transfer a call from your iPhone or iPad to your MacBook Air. To transfer a FaceTime call from your MacBook Air to your iPhone or iPad, hit the switch icon in the upper left corner of your device, then tap⬜️ it once more.

Your MacBook Air should be Handoff enabled. Open System Settings, choose General from the sidebar, then pick Airdrop & Handoff. Then choose "Allow Handoff between this Mac and your iCloud devices."

Your iOS or iPadOS device should have Handoff turned on. Tap to enable Handoff after going to Settings > General > Handoff. Your device doesn't allow handoff if you can't see the choice.

Apple Watch Handoff should be enabled. Go to Settings > General in the Apple Watch app on your iPhone, then press to enable handoff.

Use Universal Clipboard on your Mac

In a short amount of time, quickly copy content from one gadget and paste it onto another one that is close by. All Mac, iPhone, iPad, and iPod touch devices that are signed in with the same Apple ID and have Handoff, Wi-Fi, and Bluetooth turned on are able to access the contents of your clipboard through Wi-Fi.

You must have an iPhone, iPod touch, or iPad with iOS 10 or later installed in order to utilize Universal Clipboard.

Apply to all apps. On your Mac, iPhone, iPad, and iPod touch, you may copy and paste text, pictures, photos, and videos between any apps that allow copy and paste.

Copy and paste files. Using Universal Clipboard, you may rapidly transfer files from one Mac to another. On your MacBook Air, you can copy a file and then paste it into a Finder window, a Mail message, or any other app that supports copy and paste that is close by. On both computers, you must be logged in using the same Apple ID.

Universal Control

With Universal Control, you may operate many devices with a single keyboard, mouse, or trackpad. You may work across up to three devices when you drag the cursor from the edge of your MacBook Air screen to your iPad or another Mac.

Note: To utilize Universal Control, your Mac must be running macOS version 12.3 or later, and your iPad must be running iPadOS 15.4 or more.

Evaluate your connections. Your Mac's Universal Control uses Bluetooth to find an additional device and Wi-Fi to connect it. Ensure that Bluetooth is enabled and that Wi-Fi is active on each device. Aside from that, make sure Handoff is enabled in the iPad's Settings > General > AirPlay & Handoff and the MacBook Air's General settings. The same Apple ID must be used on both devices, and two-factor authentication must be enabled. You can connect your gadgets using Control Center once these settings are accurate. Select Screen Mirroring from the Control Center menu bar on your Mac, then select a device from the list beneath Link Keyboard and Mouse.

Alternate between screens. On your Mac, drag the pointer to the right or left edge of the screen that is closest to your iPad using your mouse or trackpad, stop, and then move the pointer just a little bit past the edge of the screen. Continue pointing the pointer at the iPad screen after a border form at the edge.

Drop and drag. Drag the text, image, or other object you wish to move to the desired location on your other device after selecting it. You could drag an Apple Pencil sketch from your iPad to the Keynote software on your MacBook Air, for instance. Additionally, you can copy content from one device and paste it into another.

Use the same keyboard. When the insertion point is blinking and the pointer is in a document or another area where you can input text, you can start typing.

Sidecar on your Mac

With Sidecar, you may use your iPad as a tablet input device for Mac programs and as a second display for your Mac. Give yourself more room to work, use the Apple Pencil to doodle, annotate PDFs and screenshots, and other things.

Note: iPad models running iPadOS 13.1 or later and supporting the Apple Pencil can use Sidecar.

Connect and set up. Within ten meters (32 feet) of your Mac, you can use your iPad wirelessly, or you can use a cable to connect your iPad to your Mac to keep it charged. Go to Apple menu > System Settings, choose Displays, and then select your iPad from the Add Display pop-up menu to configure your iPad as a second display. Later, you can connect to your iPad through Control Center Display area. In Control

Center, select the Sidecar button ⬛ to unpair your iPad from your Mac. On your iPad, you can also tap ▱ on the sidebar.

Set the Sidecar's options. Click Displays in System Settings, then select the name of your iPad. Then, you can choose the Sidecar settings for your iPad, including whether it is the primary display or simply a mirror of your Mac, if the sidebar and Touch bar are displayed and where, and whether you can double-tap with the Apple Pencil to access tools.

Note: that these options are not available in the Display settings if your iPad has not been configured.

Mirror or extend your desktop. You can drag programs and documents between your Mac and iPad when you connect your iPad, which makes it an automatic extension of your Mac desktop. Move your cursor over the Sidecar button ⬛ in Control Center, click the right arrow that appears above the button, then choose Mirror Built-in Retina Display to make your Mac screen visible on both devices (mirror the display).

By selecting Use As Separate Display from the menu, you can extend your desktop once more.

Tip: You may configure Display settings to always appear in the menu bar for quick access to the Sidecar choices. To choose whether to always display the Displays icon in the menu bar or only when it is active, go to System Settings > Control Center and click the pop-up menu next to Displays. The Display icon in the menu bar changes to while Sidecar is running and your iPad is plugged in.

Use the Apple Pencil. Draw and design precisely in your preferred professional programs. To use the Apple Pencil, simply drag the window from your Mac to your iPad. You may also annotate PDFs, screenshots, and pictures using the Apple Pencil.

The Apple Pencil's pressure and tilt functions are limited to apps that have sophisticated stylus support.

Utilize the sidebar shortcuts. On your iPad, use the sidebar to easily access frequently used buttons and features. Use the keyboard shortcuts, display or conceal the menu bar, Dock, and keyboard by tapping the buttons.

Whether you have a Touch Bar or not, use the controls. Whether or not your Mac has a Touch Bar, the controls for apps that support it are displayed at the bottom of the iPad's display.

Continuity Camera on your Mac

You may use your iPhone as an additional camera for your Mac by using Continuity Camera on your Mac. You can use the camera on your iPhone to make video calls, capture pictures, add them to documents, and save them to your Mac.

Note: An iPhone XR or newer is required to use Continuity Camera as a webcam. You need an iPhone, iPod touch, or iPad with iOS 12.1, or later, installed in order to use Continuity Camera to share photographs. Make sure the Wi-Fi and Bluetooth are turned on and that both your MacBook Air and your iOS or iPadOS device are logged in using the same Apple ID.

Wirelessly operate. When your iPhone is nearby after you set up Continuity Camera, your Mac can instantly switch to using it as a camera. If you'd prefer, you can also connect via a wired connection.

Use the microphone on your iPhone. Additionally, you can connect your iPhone to your Mac as a microphone. When making a video call, utilize FaceTime's Video menu to choose your iPhone or the app's settings to use your iPhone's microphone. To choose your iPhone as your system microphone, go to System Settings and select Audio.

Implement video effects. You can employ video effects like Center Stage, Portrait mode, Studio Light, and Desk View when making video calls on your iPhone. While Studio Light darkens the background and highlights your face, Center Stage keeps the camera centered on you as you move, and Portrait mode blurs the background while maintaining the focus on you. You can show both your face and what's in front of you when you use Desk View with your iPhone as a webcam for your MacBook Air. Click Control Center in the menu bar, then choose the desired effect, to use video effects. Center Stage and Desk View require an iPhone 11 or later, and Studio Light requires an iPhone 12 or later.

Add a photo or scan. Use your iPhone, iPad, or iPod touch's camera to scan documents or take pictures of surrounding objects. On your Mac, the image shows immediately. Choose where you want the image to appear in an app like Mail, Notes, or Messages, click File (or Insert) > Import From iPhone or iPad, pick "Take Photo" or "Scan Documents," and then snap the picture or scan the document on your iOS or iPadOS device. Before snapping the picture, you might need to choose your iOS or iPadOS device. Click Use Photo or Keep Scan. If you wish to try again, you can tap Retake.

Choose where you want the image to go in a program like Pages, then Control-click, pick "Import image," and take the picture. Choosing your camera beforehand may be necessary.

On an iOS or iPadOS device, move the frame until the object you wish to display is inside it, select Keep Scan, and then tap Save to take a scan. To rescan the content, tap Retake.

Wherever you want it to be in your paper, the photo or scan will appear.

Continuity Sketch and Continuity Markup on your Mac

With Continuity Sketch, you may create a sketch on your iPhone or iPad in close proximity and then immediately insert it into a Mac document, such as an email, message, document, or note. Alternatively, you can utilize Continuity Markup to edit a document on an iPad or an iOS device with your finger and then view the changes on your Mac.

Note: An iPhone, iPod touch, or iPad with iOS 13 (or later) or iPadOS 13.1 (or later) is required to use Continuity Sketch and Continuity Markup. Make sure Bluetooth and Wi-Fi are turned on and that you are logged in with the same Apple ID across all of your devices. Only apps with sophisticated stylus support provide pressure and tilt for the Apple Pencil.

Include a drawing. Place the pointer where you wish to insert a sketch in a program like Mail, Notes, or Messages. Select Add Sketch after selecting File (or Insert) > Import from iPhone or iPad. Draw a sketch with your finger or the Apple Pencil (on an iPad that supports it) on your iOS device or iPad, and then press Done. The drawing displays on your Mac where you put the pointer. You can annotate or enlarge the sketch depending on where it is placed.

Mark up the paper. With Continuity Markup, you can annotate PDFs, screenshots, and photos on an iPad , iPhone, or iPod touch that is close by while viewing the changes on your Mac. To read the document in Quick Look, hold down the Space bar while doing so, and then click the device icon. Click

Annotate, then select a device if both devices are in close proximity. To indicate that your device is connected, the tool can seem highlighted.

Start adding shapes or writing with your finger or the Apple Pencil (if your iPad allows it). As you make improvements on your iPad, iPhone, or iPod touch, you can watch them happen live on your Mac.

Use AirDrop on your Mac

Sharing files with nearby Mac, iPhone, iPad, and iPod touch devices is simple with AirDrop. The Apple IDs on the devices don't have to match.

A device must have a Lightning or USB-C port, iOS 7 (or later), or iPadOS 13.1 (or later) in order to use AirDrop for iOS or iPadOS. AirDrop is not supported by all older Macintosh computers.

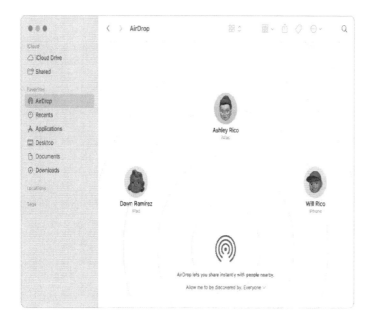

From the Finder, send a file. Select the device you want to transfer the item to by controlling-clicking the item and selecting Share > AirDrop. Alternatively, you can choose Go > AirDrop or click the Finder icon in the Dock, then select AirDrop from the sidebar on the left. Drag the file from the desktop or another Finder window to the recipient once they are visible in the window. A file can be sent to someone, and they can decide whether or not to open it.

From an app, send a file. Select the device you want to transfer the item to when using an app like Pages or

Preview, then click the Share icon ⬆️ and choose AirDrop.

Use AirDrop to limit who can send you things. You may also toggle AirDrop on or off here by clicking the Control Center button 🔘 in the menu bar, clicking AirDrop 📶, and then choosing "Contacts only" or "Everyone." The settings for the iPad, iPhone, and iPod touch are comparable.

Tip: Check that both devices have AirDrop and Bluetooth turned on and are within 30 feet (9 meters) of each other if you can't see the recipient in the AirDrop window. Try clicking "Don't see who you're looking for? " if the recipient has an older Mac."

Receive items with AirDrop. You have the option to accept or save items that are sent to you via AirDrop on your Mac. Choose to store the item to your Downloads folder or an app like Photos after clicking Accept when you see the AirDrop message and desire it. You may easily send something from one device to another, such as a photo from your iPhone, and it will be saved automatically if you have multiple devices signed in with the same iCloud account.

Passwords kept in the iCloud Keychain can be shared. With another Mac, iPhone, iPad, or iPod touch, as well as one of your contacts, you can share an account password in Safari using AirDrop. Open Settings > Passwords from the Safari menu, choose the website whose password you want to share, and then Control-click. To share the password, select "Share with AirDrop," then in the AirDrop window, pick the recipient's name or device.

Instant Hotspot on your Mac

Your Wi-Fi connection was lost. With Instant Hotspot, you may rapidly connect your MacBook Air to the internet using the Personal Hotspot on your iPhone or iPad without entering a password.

Note: In order to use Personal Hotspot, you must have an iPhone with iOS 8 (or later) or an iPad with cellular support and iPadOS 13.1 (or later).

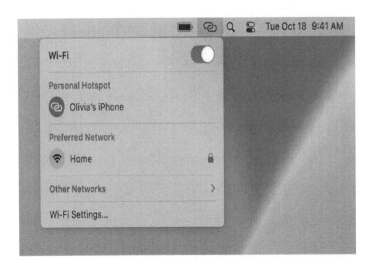

Connect to the Personal Hotspot on your device.

Click the Wi-Fi status icon in the menu bar, then select your iPhone or iPad from the list (or click Other Networks if you don't see the list). The toolbar's Wi-Fi icon transforms into . Your device doesn't need to be configured in any way for the MacBook Air to connect. Your MacBook Air disconnects from the hotspot when you aren't using it to conserve battery life.

Tip: Verify your devices are configured properly if you're asked for a password.

Check your connection's status. To determine the quality of the cellular signal, check the Wi-Fi status menu.

Phone calls and text messages on your Mac

You can make and receive calls directly from your MacBook Air if you have a Wi-Fi connection. Additionally, SMS messages can be sent and received.

Create a FaceTime call setup. Go to Settings > Phone on your iPhone (iOS 9 or later) and turn on Wi-Fi calling. Then launch FaceTime on your Mac. Select "Calls from iPhone" under General in Settings, then click "Settings."

Make a call. Click Create Link or New FaceTime after launching FaceTime on your Mac. You can share the link created by Create Link using AirDrop, Mail, Messages, Notes, or Reminders. You can input a name, email address, or phone number while using new FaceTime. In Contacts, you may also begin a FaceTime call. To find a contact in the FaceTime row, click the phone symbol 📞. Additionally, you can click a phone number in a Spotlight search or in an app like Calendar or Safari (your iPhone or iPad must be nearby and have a cellular connection).

Take a call. Click the notification that shows on your MacBook Air screen when your iPhone receives a call. If you don't have headphones on, your MacBook Air functions as a speakerphone.

Tip: Enable Do Not Disturb on your Mac to temporarily disable notifications for incoming calls, messages, and other events. Choose Focus, a time limit, and the Control Center symbol 🎛 from the menu bar.

Send and receive messages. To send text messages from your MacBook Air, use Messages. Every message shows up on your MacBook Air, iPhone, iPad, iPod touch, and Apple Watch, allowing you to reply to texts on the device that is nearest to you.

Share experiences with SharePlay

You may watch TV shows and movies, listen to music, or view material while on a FaceTime conversation with your friends and family with SharePlay. Share a film or song with your friends in Messages, start a real-time watch party, listen to new music together, or just share what's on your screen while chatting about it. On their iPhone (iOS 15 or later), iPad (iPadOS 15 or later), or Mac with macOS Monterey or later installed, your pals can take part. You can converse with your pals on a different device while watching video on Apple TV (tvOS 15 or later).

Be aware that certain SharePlay-compatible apps demand a subscription in order to use them. Not every country or location has access to every feature and piece of information.

Start by using FaceTime. You can utilize SharePlay to share an experience with your friends, family, or coworkers after starting a FaceTime chat with them. A SharePlay link can also be added to a topic in Messages. Profit from the updated FaceTime calling capabilities including grid view, spatial audio (which disperses the voices so they appear to be coming from different locations), and voice isolation (which highlights your voice and reduces background noise).

Watch together. Bring movies, TV series, online videos, and more into your group FaceTime sessions to enjoy watching films with your coworkers. Everyone's playback keeps pace if you pause, rewind, fast-forward, or jump to a different scene. With smart volume, the audio is automatically changed so you can carry on a conversation while watching.

Listen together. You can play music for your buddies during FaceTime calls or organize a dance party. Any caller may add music to the collective queue whilst listening. Everyone on the call has access to the playback settings, and by listening with smart volume, you and everyone else may talk without shouting.

Share your screen with others. To include websites, applications, and more in your FaceTime conversation, use SharePlay. Anything that shows up on your screen has the potential to be a shared experience. Together, go through vacation rentals, look for bridesmaid attire, impart knowledge, or present an impromptu slide presentation in Photos. Share your entire screen or just a single window.

Use AirPlay on your Mac

Using AirPlay screen mirroring, you can project whatever is on your MacBook Air onto a larger screen. You can also use AirPlay to broadcast material to your Mac from an iPhone, iPad, or even another Mac. Connect your HDTV to Apple TV and make sure it is connected to the same Wi-Fi network as your MacBook Air in order to use the Apple TV as a second display or to mirror the MacBook Air screen on your TV. When you want to watch a movie but want to keep your work private, you can also play web videos directly on your HDTV without displaying what is on your desktop.

Make a desktop mirror by utilizing Screen Mirroring. When AirPlay is turned on, the Control Center symbol in the menu bar turns blue; click it, select Screen Mirroring , then select your Apple TV.

When an Apple TV is connected to the same network as your Mac, you will notice an AirPlay status icon in the menu bar if your Mac supports AirPlay screen mirroring.

Peer-to-peer AirPlay allows you to use an AirPlay display in particular circumstances even if your MacBook Air is not connected to the same Wi-Fi network as your Apple TV. You need an Apple TV (3rd generation rev A, model A1469 or later) with tvOS 7.0 or later in order to enable peer-to-peer AirPlay.

Send files from other devices to your Mac. While the content is being played on your other devices, you can watch videos, listen to music, and more on your Mac. By using your Mac as a secondary display for apps that allow it, including Keynote and Photos, you may extend the display of your iPhone or iPad by mirroring it on your computer. You may stream music or podcasts to your Mac via AirPlay 2, or you can utilize it as a second speaker for multiroom audio. Any Apple device may be used with your Mac, and connecting two devices that use the same Apple ID is much simpler.

Show no sign of your desktop while playing web videos. Click the AirPlay symbol next to a web video you want to play, then choose your Apple TV from the list that appears.

Advice: To get the best possible picture, modify the desktop size if the image doesn't fit your HDTV screen when you mirror the screen. When the video's AirPlay icon is clicked, select a choice under "Match Desktop Size To."

At apple.com or your nearby Apple Store, you may purchase Apple TV on its own.

Unlock your Mac and approve tasks with Apple Watch

You may accept authentication chores, such as entering passwords, accessing notes and settings, and allowing installations, while wearing your Apple Watch, which will immediately unlock your MacBook Air. To ensure secure communication between your Apple Watch and MacBook Air, these capabilities employ powerful encryption.

To use Apple Watch's Auto Unlock and Approve using feature:

- Use the same Apple ID to log in on your Mac and Apple Watch.
- To automatically unlock your Mac, make sure your Apple Watch is unlocked and running watchOS 3 or later; accepting authentication requests requires watchOS 6 or later.
- Enable two-factor authentication by doing as follows.

Set Up Two-Factor Authentication for your Apple ID: Open System Settings, click your Apple ID in the sidebar, choose Password & Security, then select Set Up Two-Factor Authentication to enable two-factor authentication for your Apple ID.

Be careful to select "Disable automatic login" as well. (FileVault users won't see this option, but they can still use the "Auto Unlock" and "Approve with Apple Watch" functions.

Set up Auto Unlock: If your Apple Watch has watchOS 6 or later installed, click Security & Privacy, then click General, and select "Use your Apple Watch to unlock apps and your Mac." If your Apple Watch has watchOS 3 to watchOS 5 installed, select "Allow your

Apple Watch to unlock your Mac." You can't approve authentication tasks unless your Apple Watch has watchOS 6 or later installed. To set up Auto Unlock, sign in on all of your devices with the same Apple ID, then open System Settings on your MacBook Air.

Note: You authenticate your Apple Watch with a passcode every time you put it on, so there are no more steps required after you input your passcode for these capabilities to function.

Skip the sign in: With your verified Apple Watch on your wrist, approach your sleeping MacBook Air without having to sign in. Lift the lid or press a key to wake it up; Apple Watch unlocks it so you can start working straight away.

Approve with Apple Watch: You can browse your passwords in Safari, approve app installations, access a locked note, and more (needs watchOS 6). If you're asked for a password, double-click the side button on your Apple Watch to confirm your password on your Mac.

Use Apple Pay on your Mac

You can use Apple Pay on your MacBook Air to quickly, securely, and privately make purchases online. Your Apple Card information and any other credit or debit card information are never saved by Apple or given to the merchant while using Apple Pay. In Safari, seek for an Apple Pay checkout option when you order online. Use your Apple Watch, iPhone, or Touch ID to confirm the transaction.

Not all nations or regions now offer Apple Pay or Apple Card.

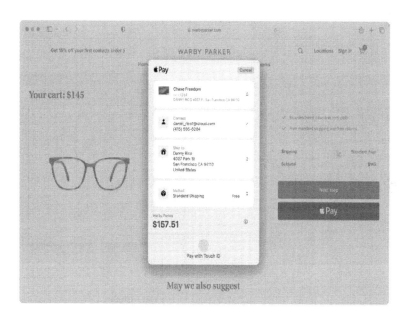

Configure Apple Pay. There is no additional setup needed with Apple Pay because it uses your Apple Card or any credit or debit cards that you have already registered on your iPhone or Apple Watch. The Apple ID you use for your MacBook Air must also be logged in on an iPhone or Apple Watch that supports Apple Pay. For purchases on your Mac, the default payment card, shipping method, and contact details that are configured on your iPhone or Apple Watch are used. You can set up debit or credit cards in the Wallet & Apple Pay settings under System Settings if you don't already have them there on your iPhone or Apple Watch.

Make a purchase using Touch ID. On your MacBook Air, you are prompted to configure Apple Pay during setup. To authenticate and finish your transaction after selecting Apple Pay on a website, place your finger lightly on the Touch ID sensor.

Purchase something using your iPhone or Apple Watch. To confirm the payment, use Face ID, Touch ID, the passcode on your iPhone, or double-click the side button on your unlocked Apple Watch after clicking the Apple Pay button on the website. The Apple ID you use for your MacBook Air must also be logged in on an iPhone or Apple Watch that supports Apple Pay.

In the Wallet & Apple Pay settings of System Settings, you can manage your Apple Card and add or remove payment cards.

Use AirPrint on your Mac

You can print photographs and documents from your Mac without downloading and installing printer drivers if your printer supports AirPrint.

AirPrint enables wireless printing to:

- A printer on your Wi-Fi network that supports AirPrint
- A printer shared by another Mac on your Wi-Fi network or a network printer.
- A printer attached to an AirPort base station's USB port

To an AirPrint printer, print. When printing from an app, select a printer from the Nearby Printers list by clicking the Printer pop-up option in the Print dialog.

Can't seem to locate the printer you need? Make that your MacBook Air and it are both linked to the same Wi-Fi network. Try adding it if it's connected and you still can't see it by opening System Settings, selecting Printers & Scanners from the sidebar, and then clicking Add Printer, Scanner, or Fax on the right. (You might need to use a USB connection and an adaptor, if necessary, to temporarily connect the printer to your MacBook Air.)

Chapter 3

Apps on your MacBook Air

Your MacBook Air comes with a selection of fantastic apps for daily tasks like online browsing, keeping in touch with friends and family via Messages and FaceTime, and managing your schedule. To help you get started being creative and productive, it also includes apps like Photos, Apple Music, Apple Podcasts, the Apple TV app, Pages, Numbers, and Keynote.

Not all macOS apps are accessible in all countries or all languages.

I can't find my apps. The Applications folder in your Finder window is where you may find the apps. You can drag programs to your Dock or access them directly from the folder. You may find Disk Utility , Keychain Access , Migration Assistant , VoiceOver Utility , and other helpful programs in the programs subfolder of this folder.

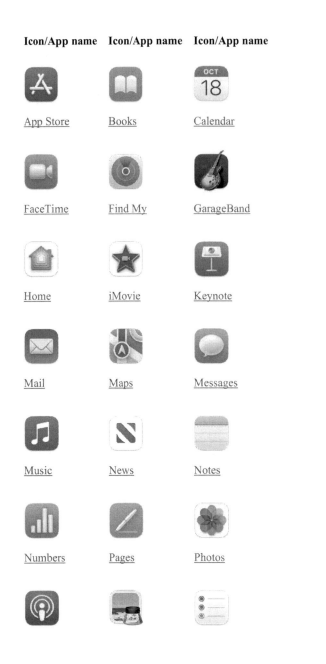

Icon/App name	Icon/App name	Icon/App name
App Store	Books	Calendar
FaceTime	Find My	GarageBand
Home	iMovie	Keynote
Mail	Maps	Messages
Music	News	Notes
Numbers	Pages	Photos

The apps that come with your Mac are listed below.

The Applications folder contains additional applications that are not included in the table above, such as Calculator ▦ , Chess ♟ , Clock 🕐 , Contacts ◻ , TextEdit ▱ , Weather ☁ , and others.

Identify other apps. For practically everything you want to do, search for and download an app by clicking the App Store icon 🄰 in the Dock.

Find support for any software. When using an app, select the Help option from the menu bar at the top of the screen.

**App Store**

To browse and download programs, as well as to obtain the most recent updates for your apps, search the App Store.

Discover the ideal app. Are you certain of what you want? Enter the name of the program in the search box, then hit Return. Applications that you download from the App Store show up on Launchpad automatically. Alternately, you can go through the results by selecting a sidebar option, such as Create, Work, or Play, and browsing through new apps.

Not all nations or areas have access to Apple Arcade.

Dial Siri. Something along the lines of "Find apps for kids."

Click a tab to browse apps.

Search for an app by name.

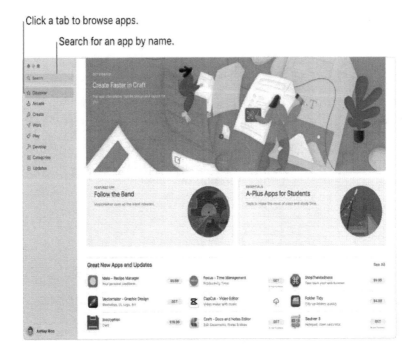

To download free apps, simply sign in with your Apple ID in the App Store by clicking Sign In at the bottom of the sidebar. Click Sign In, then click Create Apple ID if you don't already have one. If you already have an Apple ID but can't remember your password, click "Forgot Apple ID or password?" to get it back. To purchase paid apps, you must also create an account with payment details.

Utilize the iPad and iPhone apps on your Mac. Your MacBook Air is compatible with many iPhone and iPad apps. Your Mac displays any available apps that you've already bought for your iPhone or iPad. Check the Mac version of any apps you're interested in in the App Store.

Game on. Learn how to subscribe to Apple Arcade, find games you can play, find ones that are well-liked by your Game Center friends, see your achievement progress, and more by selecting the Arcade tab. Games that you download from the App Store are always simple to access, even with a gaming controller, because they automatically appear in the Games folder in Launchpad.

Save your game action. By pressing the share button on supported third-party game controllers, you can record a 15-second video clip of gameplay that you can revisit later or store as a record of special gaming moments.

Invite your friends to the game. It is simple to invite your most recent Messages friends and groups to join games that support Game Center using the new multiplayer buddy picker. In the friend request inbox, view incoming invitations and requests.

Get the latest app updates. There are updates available if the App Store icon in the Dock has a badge. To access the App Store, click the icon, then select Updates from the sidebar.

You have
available updates.

**Books**

Use Apple Books to read, catalog, and buy new books for your Mac's book and audiobook collection. Establish reading objectives and keep a record of both your current reading and your desired reading.

Not all nations or areas have access to Apple Books.

A bookshelf on your Mac. Reading Now displays books that you've already begun reading at the top. Browse or search every book in your library, or select a category from the sidebar's Book Store or Audiobook Store to discover new books and other publications. Simply login in with your Apple ID (select Account > login in) to make a purchase. Additionally, books can be purchased directly from search results.

Ask Siri. Tell them to "find books by Jane Austen."

Type what you're looking for.

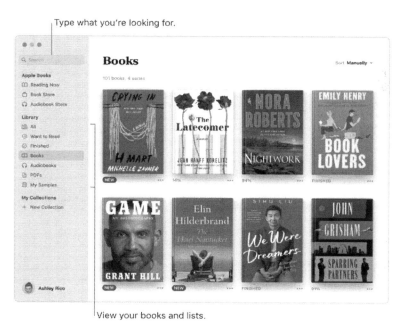

View your books and lists.

Make reading targets. Make reading goals for each day to spur yourself on to additional reading. If you wish to set a greater target than the default of 5 minutes each day, click ⚏ in Reading Now's Reading Goals area and select a new one. You can disable this and delete reading goal information in the Books settings.

Add highlights, notes, and bookmarked pages.

Click ⬛ to bookmark a page (click the bookmark again to delete the bookmark) after moving your pointer to the top of the book you're reading. When the controls are shown, click ⬛ the bookmark to open the page you just bookmarked. Select the text, then select a highlight color or Add Note from the pop-up menu to add notes or highlights. Show the controls, then click ⬛ to read your notes later.

Never misplace your markups or your location. As long as you're signed in with the same Apple ID across all of your devices, your purchased books, collections, bookmarks, highlights, and notes, as well as the page you're currently reading, are immediately accessible on your Mac, iOS devices, and iPadOS devices.

Tip: Change the theme to night to make it easier to read in dim light. Select Night under View > Theme, or click the Appearance iconAA, then select the black circle. Not all texts embrace the theme of night.

Use Night theme.

 **Calendar**

With Calendar, you'll never forget an appointment. Create numerous calendars to keep track of your hectic schedule, and manage them all in one location.

Create occasions. Double-click anywhere in a day, or click  to add a new event. Double-click the event, select the Add Invitees area, and then enter the recipient's email address. When your invitees respond, the calendar notifies you.

Dial Siri. Just say something like, "Set up a meeting with Mark at nine in the morning."

Tip: A helpful hint is that Calendar provides a map, an estimated journey time and departure time, as well as the weather prediction, if you add a place to an event.

Every aspect of your life should have a calendar.
Make distinct calendars with their own colors, such as
those for work, home, and school. Create a calendar
by selecting File > New Calendar, then Control-click
each calendar to select a different color.

Calendars for holidays should be added. View
holiday schedules for various parts of the world. Select
a holiday calendar you want to add by selecting File >
New Holiday Calendar.

View every calendar you have or a select few. To
view a list of all of your calendars, click the Calendars
button; then, click the calendars you want to view in
the pop-up window.

Use Focus to filter your calendars. Select which calendars to display during a specific Focus. Have a calendar with assignment due dates, for instance, that only displays while someone is studying. Select Focus from the sidebar by selecting Apple Menu > System Settings. Choose Add Filter from the list of Focus Filters after selecting a focus on the right.

Share with friends and across your devices. You can share calendars with other iCloud users when you're logged in, and your calendars are kept up to date on all of your Macintosh computers, iOS devices, iPadOS devices, and Apple Watch that are signed in with the same Apple ID.

FaceTime

Make video and voice calls to a friend or group of friends with FaceTime on your Mac. FaceTime allows you to make calls between your iPhone and MacBook Air and transfer calls between them, as well as use your iPhone's camera as a webcam.

Dial Siri. Say something like, "Call Sharon on FaceTime."

Call someone on FaceTime. Make FaceTime video calls on your Mac using the built-in FaceTime HD camera. Click New FaceTime, type the person's name, phone number, or email address, and then click FaceTime. Make an audio-only call by selecting FaceTime Audio from the pop-up menu if making a video call is not practical. You have the option to join FaceTime with video or only audio when you receive an invitation.

Tip: You can move the tiny picture-in-picture window to any corner of the FaceTime window while a video call is active.

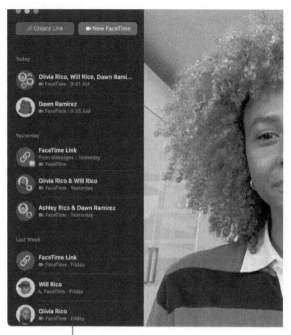

List of recent calls

Pass the FaceTime call off. When you're away from home, start a FaceTime call on your iPhone, then transfer it to your Mac once you're back at your workstation. You may also make a FaceTime call from your Mac and then switch to another device if necessary. Bluetooth headphones that are plugged in change as well.

Click ⬜️🎥 Switch in the menu bar of your Mac, then click Join in the FaceTime window on your MacBook Air to transfer a FaceTime call from your iPhone or iPad to the laptop. To transfer a FaceTime call from your

MacBook Air to your iPhone or iPad, hit the switch icon in the upper left corner of your device, then tap  it once more.

Use the webcam on your iPhone. Utilize the iPhone camera's capabilities for FaceTime calls on your Mac. Keep your iPhone steady, in landscape mode—for instance, by setting it on a stand—with the screen off and the back cameras pointed in your direction. Choose your iPhone from the list under FaceTime > Video on your Mac. If you have an iPhone 11 or later, you can use Center Stage, which keeps the call centered on you even as you move. By selecting Video Effects from the menu bar and then selecting another option, such as Portrait mode, you can select different video effects.

Display the area in front of you. When you connect your iPhone to your MacBook Air as a camera using Desk View, you can share both what's in front of you and your face. Set up your iPhone as a webcam, then click Desk View in the upper right corner of the FaceTime window on your Mac to share with Desk View during a call. Alternatively, select Desk View by clicking Video Effects in the menu bar. Click Share Desk View after using the options to align your desk with the window. Click on the Desk View window to stop sharing Desk View. iPhone 11 and later support Desk View.

Note: Your iPhone, iPad, and Mac need Bluetooth, WiFi, and Handoff turned on. Your iPhone, iPad, and Mac need Continuity Camera turned on in AirPlay & Handoff settings on your iPhone or iPad, and you must be signed into your iPhone, iPad, and MacBook Air with the same Apple ID.

FaceTime your group members. In a group call, you can connect with up to 32 individuals. Make a special link and distribute it to the group. To create a link, click. Share the link directly with friends in Mail or Messages by copying it to your clipboard. On non-Apple devices, you can now join FaceTime calls by clicking a link.

To arrange a call for later, include a FaceTime link in a Calendar event.

Live captions and identification of sign language. When a participant in a Group FaceTime call is using sign language, FaceTime recognizes this and highlights the individual. FaceTime Live subtitles recognize what is being spoken and provide real-time subtitles for the speaker who is now speaking.

Observe while also listening. On a Mac, utilize SharePlay to watch and listen together. During a FaceTime call, your screen can also be shared. To begin, click the SharePlay icon .

Be aware that certain SharePlay-compatible apps demand a subscription in order to use them. Not every country or location has access to every feature and piece of information.

Call a friend. Use FaceTime to place calls from your Mac if you have an iPhone with iOS 8 or later. Just make sure the feature is enabled on both your Mac and iPhone and that they are both signed in with the same Apple ID account. (Open FaceTime on your Mac, go to FaceTime > Settings, and pick "Calls from iPhone.")

To make or receive calls on your MacBook Air, you must be connected to the internet and the same Wi-Fi network on both devices.

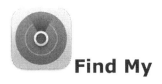 **Find My**

You can use the Find My app to find your loved ones, Apple devices, and friends.

Locate your friends, devices, or items.

Not all regions or languages have access to Find My features.

Describe places to pals. To let loved ones know where you are, click Share My Location in the People list. You have the option to publish your current location for a short period of time—say, an hour—or for as long as you choose. You may also request to be followed by a buddy so you can see their whereabouts on a map and receive detailed directions to get there.

Configure location notifications. Automatically notify friends when you enter or leave a particular location. Set up alerts for the departure and arrival of your friends as well. Click Me in the People list, then scroll to Notifications About You to see all the notifications your friends have created about your location.

Receive alerts when you drop something off. Create separation alerts on your iPhone, iPad, or iPod touch to inform you when you leave a device behind, such as a MacBook Air. Click ⓘ on the device, then select Notify When Left Behind, and then follow the on-screen directions to configure separation alerts for that particular device.

Protect a stolen device. Use Find My to find lost items like your Mac, iPhone, or AirPods and to keep them safe. To find a device on the map, click it in the Devices list. Click ⓘ to view choices like remotely wiping the device, marking the device as lost to prevent others from accessing your personal data, and playing a sound on it to help you find it.

Find devices, including those that are not online. When your device is not connected to Wi-Fi or a cellular network, Find My uses Bluetooth signals from neighboring Apple devices to find it. These signals, which aid in locating your missing gadget without jeopardizing privacy, are anonymous and encrypted. For Mac computers running macOS 12 or later, iPhone and iPod touch devices running iOS 15 or later, and iPads running iPadOS 15 or later, you can even locate a device that has been wiped.

Locate a family member's gadget. If you're a part of a Family Sharing group and a family member is sharing their location with you, you can utilize Find My to help locate their device.

Find commonplace objects. If you can't find something, attach an AirTag on something like your keychain so you can find it easily. To locate items using your Mac, click the Items tab in Find My, then pick an item in the list to view its location on the map. To register an AirTag and compatible third-party items to your Apple ID, use your iOS or iPadOS device. You can view the item's last known location and get notified when it is found if the item cannot be found. For an item with a note and phone number, you can even activate Lost Mode.

 GarageBand

An app for composing, recording, and sharing music is called GarageBand. Your own home recording studio is equipped with everything you need to start learning an instrument, writing music, or recording music.

Make a fresh undertaking. Starting with a song template, choosing a tempo, key, and other choices, followed by clicking Record, will allow you to begin playing. Create your tune using loops and various tracks, for instance. To find out what something is and how it works, click Quick Help and keep the pointer over the object.

Bring the music in. Using Loops, you may easily include drums and other instruments in your production. Select a loop using the Loop Browser Instrument, Genre, or Descriptor filters, then drag it into an open space in the Tracks section. Using a straightforward set of settings, you may adjust Loops to fit your song.

Make a voice recording. Pick the microphone under Audio after selecting Track > New Track. To configure the input, output, and monitoring options, click the triangle next to Details, then click Create. To begin or stop recording, click the Play ▶ or Record buttons ●, respectively.

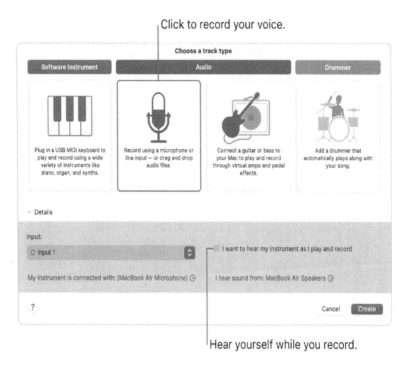

Click to record your voice.

Hear yourself while you record.

Home

You can quickly and securely manage all of your HomeKit accessories from your Mac using the Home app.

Whole-house view. With cameras, scenes, and accessories organized by room, the revamped Home page lets you see your entire house at a glance. You can easily access categories and rooms thanks to a redesigned sidebar style.

Accessories command. The Home app shows tiles with icons for accessories. Color-coded accessory categories make them easy to spot, and you can pick which tiles to enlarge so they stand out more on the Home tab. To operate an accessory tile, simply click on it. You can use it to lock or unlock a door, open or close blinds, and more. Additionally, you can change a light's brightness or a thermostat's setpoint temperature.

Categories. You may easily access all the necessary accessories arranged by room using the categories for Lights, Climate, Security, Speakers and TVs, and Water, as well as additional in-depth status information.

Categories

Click an accessory to control it.

Share Access. Family members can control items in your house using the house app on their own Apple devices if you share it with them.

Set up a scene. Make a scene that enables all of your accessories to cooperate under a single command. Make a "Good Night" scene, for instance, where you lock the door, close the blinds, and turn off all the lights before you go to bed. Click ✛ Add scenario, then click to create a scenario.

Look at your cameras. To record footage and access it from anywhere, connect your home security cameras with the Home app. The Home tab prominently

138

displays up to nine camera views and is end-to-end encrypted.

Secure Video for HomeKit. Video from home security cameras can be stored in iCloud without using up any of your available storage. Establish activity zones within a camera's field of view to record video or receive alerts only when motion is noticed there. Face Recognition enables security cameras and doorbells to recognize people you've tagged in the Photos app or the Home app as recent visitors in addition to people, animals, package delivery, and vehicle recognition. A HomeKit-compatible security camera, a HomeKit-enabled security camera, and an iPad, Apple TV, or HomePod acting as a home hub are requirements for HomeKit Secure Video.

Intelligent lighting. To increase comfort and productivity, program your smart light bulbs to change the color temperature automatically as the day progresses. Warm colors help you wake up, cool colors keep you focused and attentive during the day, and no blue light at night helps you wind down. (A home hub is required for adaptive lighting.

iMovie

With a few simple clicks, you can create stunning movies and Hollywood-style trailers from your personal recordings with iMovie.

Import a video, and iMovie will create a new library and event for you. You can import video from your iPhone, iPad, or iPod touch, from a camera, or from media files existing on your Mac.

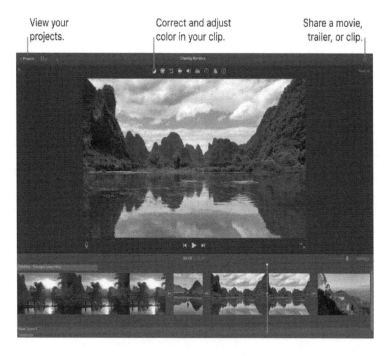

View your projects.　　Correct and adjust color in your clip.　　Share a movie, trailer, or clip.

Use the FaceTime HD camera on your Mac to record video and add it to your project. To get started, choose an event from the sidebar, click Import in the toolbar, then choose FaceTime HD Camera. To stop recording, click the Record button.

To get started, click the New button $+$, click Trailer, select a template from the Trailer window, then click Create. Add the cast and credits in the Outline tab, and add your own photos and videos in the Storyboard tab. To create clever trailers, complete with animated graphics and soaring soundtracks, just add photos and video clips.

Click Play to preview the trailer.

Using a handheld camera can result in shaky video, but you can stabilize the video to make the playback more fluid by selecting the clip in the timeline, selecting the

Stabilization button , and then selecting Stabilize Shaky Video.

 **Keynote**

With Activity Stream, it's simpler than ever to collaborate on a Keynote presentation and keep track of every change along the way. With Keynote, you can create professional, cutting-edge presentations by starting with one of the more than 30 predesigned themes and customizing it by adding text, new objects, and changing the color scheme.

Visually organize your presentation by clicking on each slide to view it in the main window, dragging a slide to reorder it, or selecting a slide and pressing the Delete key to get rid of it.

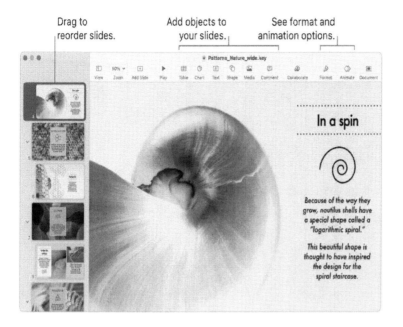

Drag to reorder slides.

Add objects to your slides.

See format and animation options.

Collaborate in Messages: Click the Share button in the menu bar, make sure Collaborate is selected, then click Messages. Choose the name of the group you want to add as participants. You can send an invitation to collaborate in Messages, and everyone on the thread is automatically added to the Keynote presentation.

Work together in real time with Activity Stream, a thorough list in the sidebar allowing you to see revisions and comments made by collaborators on a Keynote presentation, who has been added to the Keynote presentation or any other file management changes, and it's easy to monitor each update.

To practice your presentation, select Play > Rehearse Slideshow. You will see each slide, your notes, and a clock to help you stay on schedule.

See how you're doing on time.

Remind yourself
of key points to make.

Present in any situation. Create an interactive presentation that the audience controls; control your presentation remotely using your iPhone, iPad, or even your Apple Watch; and more. Present in person using an external display and use your Mac to view upcoming slides, presenter notes, a clock, and a timer. Present during a videoconference.

Share your presentation. Select Share > Send a Copy to send a copy via mail, messages, airdrop, or even social media. If your manager wants to review your presentation or you want to share it with others on a conference call.

By selecting the object on the slide, clicking Animate in the toolbar, Action in the sidebar, and Add an Effect, you may draw viewers in and grab their attention.

You can add a video to your presentation by clicking the area where you want it to appear, selecting the Media button from the toolbar, choosing Movies, finding the desired movie, and dragging it onto your slide.

Mail

The majority of well-known email services, including iCloud, Gmail, Yahoo Mail, and AOL Mail, are compatible with Mail, which enables you to manage all of your email accounts from a single app.

One-stop email: Set up Mail with all of your accounts so you can view all of your messages in one spot by selecting Mail > Add Account if you're sick of having to sign in to various websites to check your email accounts.

For example, tell Siri to "Email Laura about the trip."

macOS Ventura includes a new smart search that provides more accurate results, is aware when you make typos, and searches for synonyms for your search terms. Smart search also allows you to see a richer view of shared content and more as you search for email messages. Type in the search field to see suggestions for messages that best match your query.

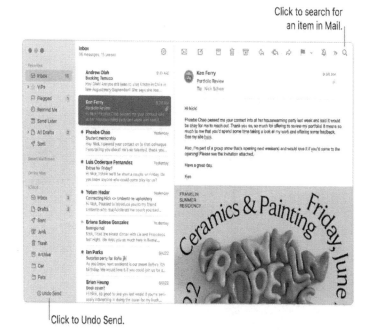

Click to search for an item in Mail.

Click to Undo Send.

You may manage your messages, see only the messages you wish to see in your inbox, mute excessively busy email threads, and unsubscribe from mailing lists directly in Mail. You can block messages from particular senders by transferring their messages directly to the Trash.

When creating an email, click the drop-down menu next to the Send button and choose one of the suggested times in the list or Send Later to specify a specific day and time. With macOS Ventura, you may plan an email to be sent at the ideal time.

Undo Send: Click Undo Send at the bottom of the sidebar in Mail within 10 seconds of sending an email to quickly unsend it before it reaches the recipient's inbox. You can also set a custom time limit by going to Mail Settings > Composing and selecting an option in the pop-up menu next to the Undo Send Delay option.

Mail can intelligently move sent email messages that did not receive a response to the top of your inbox so you can quickly send a follow-up. Mail warns you if you fail to include a crucial aspect of your message, such a recipient.

Get reminded: Control-click any email in your inbox, choose Remind Me, then choose the date and time you would want to be reminded, and the message will reappear at the top of your inbox. To be reminded about an email that you opened but didn't get back to, click the Remind Me button.

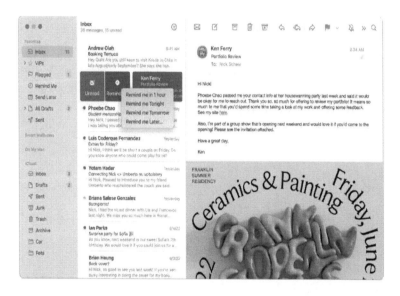

When you get a message with a new email address or event, simply click Add in the message to add it to Contacts or Calendar. Force click an address to see a preview of the location, which you can open in Maps.

Protect your privacy by turning on Privacy Protection, which stops email senders from learning information about your Mail activity and hides your IP address so they can't connect it to your other online activity or pinpoint your location. You can enable Privacy Protection in Mail Settings > Privacy by checking the box next to Protect Mail Activity.

Hide My Email address. With an iCloud+ subscription, you can generate a random, one-of-a-kind email address whenever you need one (for instance, when filling out a form on a website), with no restriction on the number of addresses you can use. You can create, manage, or disable a Hide My Email address at any time in iCloud settings on your Mac or in Account Settings on iCloud.com. When you create a Hide My Email address for a site, you can send and receive messages without having to share your real email address and have that correspondence forwarded to the email address associated with your Apple ID.

Translate quickly. Choose the text you wish to translate, Control-click it, then select Translate before selecting a language. To translate text you've typed, select "Replace with Translation."

On your Mac, select Apple Menu > System Settings, then click General in the sidebar to download additional languages so you can work offline. Go to Language & Region and then, at the bottom, choose Translation Languages. Not every language is offered.

Make any message your own. With just one click, add images or emoji. Use your photo library or your iPhone or iPad to shoot pictures. A sketch that you've created on your iPhone or iPad can also be added.

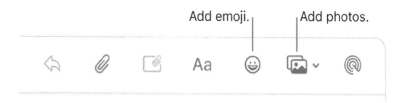

Add emoji. Add photos.

Full-screen mode. To make it simple to refer to another message in your inbox while you type, Mail's full-screen mode automatically opens windows for new messages in Split View on the right.

Utilize Focus to filter your inbox. To get the messages that matter during a certain Focus, filter your inbox by accounts. For instance, turn off work email when you're not online. Select Focus from the sidebar by selecting Apple Menu > System Settings. Choose Add Filter from the list of Focus Filters after selecting a focus on the right.

Never overlook an email. The number of unread messages may be seen by looking at the Mail icon in the Dock. A notification also flashes at the top-right of the screen when a new email arrives so you may quickly preview incoming messages. (To disable notifications, open System Settings, choose Notifications in the sidebar, select Mail from the list of applications on the right, and then adjust your notification preferences.)

You have unread
messages.

 **Maps**

Maps and satellite images can be used to find locations and get directions. Utilize guidelines selected by Apple to learn about the top attractions in a city. To drop a pin, force-click a position.

Examine in depth. Maps provide extra information, such as landmarks, elevation, natural features, and other things, to help you learn more about the world around you. New city experiences on your Mac using Apple silicon provide specifics like landmarks, structures, and even trees.

Make a route plan. Plan your route, check for traffic, and view road details like turn and bus lanes with the new driving map. Plan routes with several stops and have your iPhone automatically display them, or send a buddy direction quickly using Messages.

Find your favorites and save them. Search for it and then filter the outcomes. To find out crucial details like a location's hours of operation or whether a restaurant offers takeaway, click on the name of the establishment. The locations you visit most frequently can be saved as favorites.

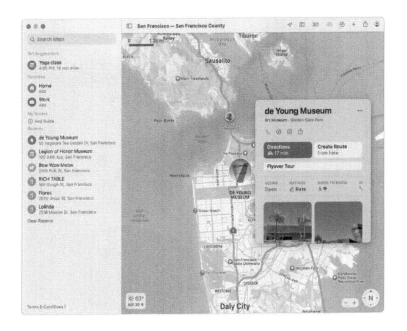

Dial Siri. Simply say, "Find coffee near me."

With guides, explore new locations. Maps offers carefully chosen suggestions from reliable brands and partners to help you find amazing places to eat, shop, and explore across the world. These guides allow you to store them and receive updates if new locations are added.

Make your own instructions. You can make your own travel guides for your favorite locations and distribute them to your loved ones. Move the cursor over My Guides in the sidebar, click ⊕ on the right, then Control-click the new guide to view a menu of options to create a new guide.

Investigate in 3D. Select cities can be viewed in 3D as you move fluidly across the streets by clicking Look Around. You can use the interactive 3D Globe on your Mac with Apple silicon to explore the splendor of the Earth's environment.

See indoor maps for locations of interest. Navigate certain airports and shopping centers. Simply zoom in to discover restrooms, arrange a meeting place for friends in the mall, identify restaurants close to your gate, and more.

Open or close the sidebar.

Take public transportation there. For a few cities, Maps offers Nearby Transit information, which includes departure times that are close to you. To discover recommended travel routes, transit prices, and projected trip times, pick 🚃 a location in the sidebar. If they are close by, pin your preferred transit routes so that they always appear at the top.

Making EV travel planning simple. When you add your electric car to your iPhone, Maps displays the locations of charging stations along your route and takes charging times into consideration when calculating your estimated time of arrival (ETA).

Route-plan your bicycle ride. The information you need to plan your bicycle route is available on maps, including elevation, traffic conditions, and the presence of strong inclines. You can send your itinerary to your iPhone after finalizing it.

Get real-time ETA updates. Maps can show you where loved ones are along their path when they share their ETA with you.

Note that not all nations or areas have access to all Maps features.

Tip: Select Show Traffic from the View menu in the menu bar to view the current traffic conditions.

 Messages

No matter the device you use, staying in touch is simple with Messages. Manage group texts, highlight favorites, browse stuff that has been shared with you, and do a lot more. Text messages can be sent using SMS/MMS or iMessage to anyone who has a Mac, iPhone, iPad, iPod touch, or Apple Watch.

Manage
a conversation,
share your
location,
and more.

With iMessage, messages are limitless. You can send an infinite number of messages to anyone who has an Apple Watch, Mac, iPhone, iPad, or Live Photo device when you sign in with your Apple ID. These devices receive encrypted messages from the Messages app that are shown in blue bubbles during conversations and are sent over iMessage.

Send SMS/MMS: If your iPhone (running iOS 8.1 or later) is signed in to Messages with the same Apple ID as your Mac, you can send and receive SMS and MMS messages on your Mac even if you aren't using iMessage. To enable Text Message Forwarding on your iPhone, go to Settings > Messages, touch Text Message Forwarding, and then tap the name of your Mac. If your Apple ID doesn't use two-factor authentication, you'll receive an activation code on your Mac; enter the code on your iPhone, then press Allow. SMS and MMS communications are not encrypted and show up in your conversations as green bubbles.

Dial Siri. Something along the lines of "Message Mom that I'll be late."

Edit and delete messages. You can edit a recently sent message up to five times within 15 minutes after sending it when conversing via Messages. You can also unsend a recently sent message for up to 2 minutes after sending it. Any sent message can be edited or sent again by control clicking it.

Unread-mark a chat. To return to a message later, when you have time to react, you can mark it as unread. In the messages list, control-click the read message, then select Mark as Unread.

Favorite dialogues should remain at the top. By dragging them there, you can pin your favorite chats to the top of the messages list. Above a pinned chat, new messages, Tapbacks, and typing indicators are displayed. The most recent participants show up around the pinned conversation when there are unread messages in a group conversation.

Control group discussions. Set a photo, Memoji, or emoji as the group image to make it simpler to recognize a group. You can address a message in a group chat to a specific person by typing their name or by using the @ sign. You can also reply inline to a question or statement that was made earlier in the conversation. You can hide chat warnings if a conversation gets too lively. Select the conversation in the list, then click the Details button ⓘ in the top-right corner of the Messages window to view choices for controlling the conversation and establish a group image. Open Settings, click General, and then check the "Notify me when my name is mentioned" box to get a notification when your name is mentioned.

Make the messages fun. Respond to messages with Memoji stickers, Tapbacks, popular GIFs, or unique effects like fluttering confetti, balloons, and more to liven up conversations. Based on your Memoji characters, Messages creates sticker packs automatically. Click the Apps button 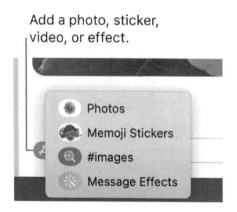, select Memoji Stickers, and then select the sticker that best captures your mood to add it to a discussion. Click and hold on a message, then select a Tapback to add. Click the Apps button , select #images or Message Effects, and then select the one you want to use to add a GIF or special effect. And keep an eye out for messages that your pals send you using Digital Touch, invisible ink, or handwriting on an Apple Watch, iPhone, or iPad.

Add a photo, sticker,
video, or effect.

Photos

Memoji Stickers

#images

Message Effects

Make a Memoji of your own. Create a unique Memoji by selecting the skin tone, freckles, hairdo, facial traits, and more. Go to Messages > Settings to set a customized Memoji as your Messages profile picture. Click Continue after selecting "Set up Name and Photo Sharing," then select "Customize." To customize your look, click the New Memoji button ⊕ and then each feature. Click Done when finished to add the Memoji to your collection of stickers. Open a discussion, select the Apps button 🅰, select Memoji Stickers ⊕, select New Memoji, then have fun designing to add more Memoji to your collection.

Send a document, image, or video. Drag files to Messages to distribute them quickly. Or easily search your Photos collection for and send pictures and videos. To add a photo to a discussion, click the Apps button 🅰, select Photos, and then click a picture. To find a certain photo, enter a term in the search bar, such as a person's name, a date, or a place.

easy to organize photos. When someone gives you many photographs, the first two or three show up as a quick-view collage, and the next four or more are combined in a stack. Use two fingers to swipe left or right on the stack of photos if you have a trackpad or Magic Mouse to view each image without opening it. To reply to, tapback, or open a photo, use the control key.

Click the Save Photo button⬇️ next to a photo to swiftly save it to Photos. Double-click the stack to view all the images in it.

Presented to You. You can access content shared with you via Messages by contacts in your Contacts whenever it suits you by visiting a new Shared with You area in the respective app. Photos, Safari, Apple News, Apple Podcasts, and the Apple TV app all display content that has been shared with you. You may view the sender of shared content in the respective applications, and with a click, access the conversation that goes with it in Messages to carry on the conversation while you enjoy the content that has been shared with you.

Tip: Click the Details ⓘ tab to view every photo in a chat.

Work on tasks together. You can invite people to work together on documents, Keynote presentations, spreadsheets in Numbers, documents in Pages, notes, and more. Click the Share icon in the program you want to use for collaboration, make sure Collaborate is chosen, then click Messages. Each member of the thread is automatically added to the document, spreadsheet, or other shared file when you select the name of the group you wish to include as participants. You may see activity updates at the top of the Messages thread whenever someone makes an adjustment.

Share your screen with others. You and a friend can share displays and even drag files to the desktop on the shared screen to open folders, create documents, and copy data. After clicking the Details option, select Screen Share.

Observe while also listening. You can watch and listen together on a Mac by joining a SharePlay session through Messages. During a FaceTime call, your screen can also be shared.

Be aware that certain SharePlay-compatible apps demand a subscription in order to use them. Not every country or location has access to every feature and piece of information.

Use Focus to filter your messages. During a certain Focus, only the messages you want to see are displayed. For a Gaming Focus, for instance, just focus on interactions with people who you typically play multiplayer games with. Select Focus from the sidebar by selecting Apple Menu > System Settings. Choose) Add Filter from the list of Focus Filters after selecting a focus on the right.

**Music**

The Apple Music app makes it simple to manage and enjoy the songs, albums, and albums you've purchased from the iTunes Store in your personal library and in the Apple Music catalog (which offers millions of tracks for on-demand listening). Click to display the current song's lyrics, upcoming tracks, and previously played tracks. Visit the iTunes Store to find the song you desire.

Your library has it. Your iTunes Store purchases, music you added from the Apple Music catalog, and music in your personal collection can all be seen and played with ease. Put your stuff through a recent additions, artist, album, or song filter.

Browse Apple Music's top tracks. To view new songs and exclusive releases from Apple songs, a music streaming service with a monthly charge, click Browse in the sidebar. Discover the ideal playlist for any situation by selecting from a wide range of playlists and more than 50 million songs available for ad-free streaming and downloading. You may now follow your favorite musicians to get updates of new releases and suggestions for other musicians you might like.

View items
in your library.

Hear the latest
Top Picks.

See what will
play next.

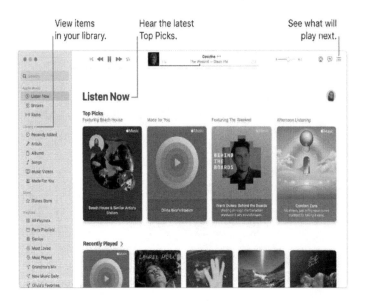

Join in the song. If accessible, clicking 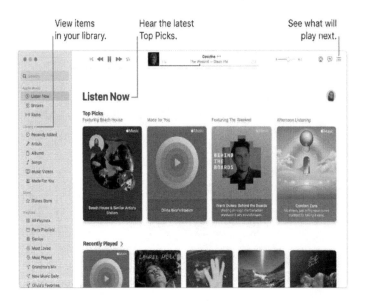 in the toolbar will bring up a panel with the song's lyrics.

Listen in. To listen to any episode from the Apple Music family of programs or to tune into Apple Music 1 live, click Radio on the sidebar. Discover the numerous stations designed for practically every musical genre.

Dial Siri. Something along the lines of "Add this song to my library."

Sync effortlessly. Directly sync your music library with the Apple Music app. When a device is connected, the Finder shows it in the sidebar. Simply drag the desired information onto your device. In the Finder, you may also backup and restore your device.

Listen together. To listen to music in real time with up to 32 pals, use SharePlay. Make a FaceTime call to gather everyone together, then click. Move the cursor over any song or album in the Music app, then press the Play button to begin listening. Everyone has access to the same playback controls, hears the same music simultaneously, and has the ability to add or rearrange songs in the shared music queue. Additionally, audio is automatically adjusted with smart volume so that you may still hear each other during a loud period.

Note: To utilize SharePlay, your Mac must be running macOS version 12.3 or later, and your iPad must be running iPadOS 15.4 or more. Some SharePlay-compatible apps demand a membership in order to function. Not every country or location has access to every feature and piece of information.

On the iTunes Store, purchase it. Click iTunes Store in the sidebar to purchase your music. (Choose Music > Settings, choose General, then check Show iTunes shop if the shop isn't shown on the sidebar.)

Use MiniPlayer to open a small floating window that you can move wherever you like so you can listen to and manage your music on your Mac while doing other things when screen space is at a premium. Select Window > MiniPlayer to launch it.

 **News**

Apple News is your one-stop shop for dependable news and information that has been edited and customized just for you. Even when offline or on other devices, you can save articles for later reading. For a single monthly fee, Apple News+ offers access to hundreds of periodicals, well-known newspapers, and premium digital publishers.

Bylines and publication dates are prominently displayed in the news feed, making it simple to peruse and confirm reports. Right from the news feed, save articles for later reading or sharing. Subscribers to News+ receive an enhanced search function and access to the News+ Library, which categorizes your content by magazines, downloadable content, newspapers, and catalog to make it simpler to find your favorites.

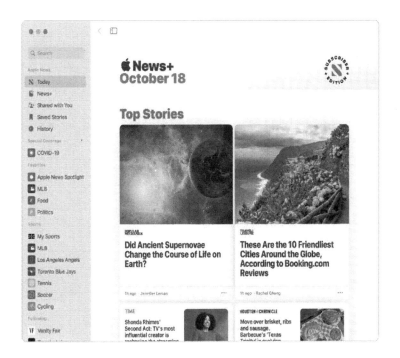

Note that not all nations or areas provide Apple News and Apple News+.

Adjust your feed. To view them in the Today feed and sidebar, follow your preferred channels and subjects. In the search box, type a news source or keyword, then click ✚ the follow button. Click Add to Favorites after Control-clicking the channel to give it more prominence in the sidebar.

Use My Sports to keep up with your favorite teams. You can access scores, schedules, and standings for the best professional and collegiate leagues on My Sports, as well as view highlights, and you may follow your favorite teams and leagues. To begin following your preferred sports, open the Today stream, scroll down to My Sports, and click Get Started.

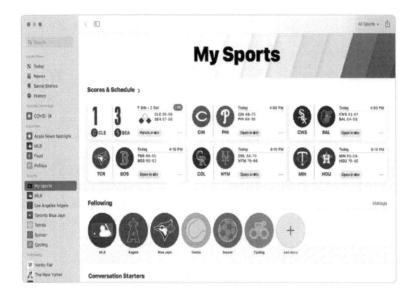

Advice: Select File > Save Story when reading an article to save it for later. Click Saved Stories up towards the top of the sidebar to read the story later. If you sign in using the same Apple ID across all of your devices, you can view articles.

Presented to You. Stories shared in Messages by friends in your contacts instantly display in the new Shared with You part of the Today feed and the Apple

News sidebar. Shared with You in both applications features stories from News and Safari, allowing you to read them wherever you are.

To save and organize articles, use Quick Note. You can add a Quick Note and tag a news story to preserve it for later if you're doing research for a project or impending vacation. Fn-Q or a specific Hot Corner can be used in News to open Quick Note and store the article link. The Quick Note can be found in the Notes app's sidebar later.

 Notes

The best place to save lengthy notes containing checklists, photos, web links, and other elements is in notes. Collaboration tools make it simple to work with others and keep informed about what's happening in your note, such as shared notes and folders, mentions, and activity view. Additionally, you can stay organized using Tags and Smart Folders, which automatically group your notes based on factors such as whether they contain attachments or checklists, when they were created or modified, and more. Additionally, it's simple to maintain all of your devices in sync with iCloud, ensuring that you always have access to your notes on any device where your Apple ID is signed in.

Dial Siri. Use a phrase like "Write a new note."

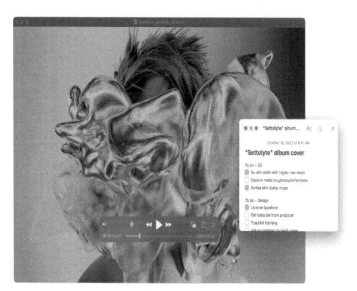

Share them, add material, and lock notes. You may rapidly add checklists, pictures, videos, sketches, tables, links, and more to your note by using the Notes toolbar. You can create a new password or use⊔ your MacBook Air login password to lock your note. You can send a copy of a note to Mail, Messages, Reminders, or AirDrop by clicking⬆, selecting Send Copy, and then selecting the sharing method.

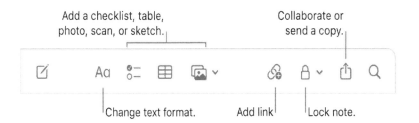

Add a checklist, table, photo, scan, or sketch.

Collaborate or send a copy.

Change text format.

Add link

Lock note.

Create a note together. In Mail or Messages, you can invite people to work together on a message, or you can copy and distribute the link. Choose Collaborate from the menu by clicking ⬆ in the toolbar, then click Messages, Mail, or Copy Link. Everyone on the thread will be added to the list immediately if you post the link in Messages. You can manage collaboration 👥 and keep track of activities once you've asked people to join.

Insert tags. To categorize and arrange the notes in the body of your note, use tags everywhere. Your tag text should be typed after the # sign. To rapidly access notes with a certain tag or tags (for example, #travel or #cooking), you can view your tags in the sidebar. Based on the same tags, custom smart folders automatically compile notes in a single location.

Employ mentions. To contact your partners on a project or in social situations, add mentions (type @

followed by a name, for example, @Leslie). They'll receive notification that they were named in a note, and they can join in right now.

Add tags and mentions.

View the summary of your collaborators' updates.

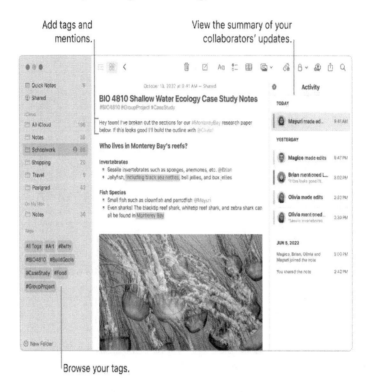

Browse your tags.

View the activity report for a note. In the Activity view on the right side of the Notes window, you may view the most recent updates regarding who has been working on a shared note. To view editor callouts, which highlight changes and display the date and time the note was changed, swipe right on the note text.

174

Utilize Smart Folders to organize. Using the filters you create, you may rapidly organize your notes using **Smart Folders.** Tags, mentions, the date a note was created or last edited, whether the note was locked or pinned, Quick Notes, and more can all be used as filters. A Smart Folder allows you to add several filters and select which ones to apply, if any at all. Click New Folder in the lower-left corner, give your folder a name, choose "Make into Smart Folder," and then enter the desired criteria.

Anywhere can add a Quick Note. On your Mac, you may use Quick Note to create notes from any program or website, and then view them in the Quick Notes category in the Notes sidebar.

Use the keyboard shortcut ⊕ -Q to create a Quick Note, or place your cursor in the lower-right corner of the screen, where Quick Note is available by default as a Hot Corner. When you highlight content on a website in Safari, you may choose Share ⬆> Add Quick Note to add the highlighted text to your note.

Note: Select Hot Corners from System Settings  >
Desktop & Dock, click Quick Notes, and then select a
separate Hot Corner to use for your Quick Notes.

Make sure your Quick Note isn't blocking what you're
watching by adjusting its size or positioning (drag the
Quick Note's corner to shrink it, or the title bar to move
it).

Make your toolbar unique. To open the Customize
Toolbar window, control-click anywhere in the tool bar.
You can customize the toolbar by dragging your
preferred items into it.

Numbers

Create beautiful and effective spreadsheets on your
Mac by using Numbers. You may get a head start when

creating budgets, invoices, team rosters, and other documents by using more than 30 templates created by Apple. Microsoft Excel spreadsheets can be opened and exported in Numbers as well. It's now simpler than ever to work together on a Numbers spreadsheet and log each update thanks to Activity Stream.

Create a template, then add the desired information. Type fresh text after selecting the template's example text. Drag a graphic file from your Mac to the placeholder picture to add graphics.

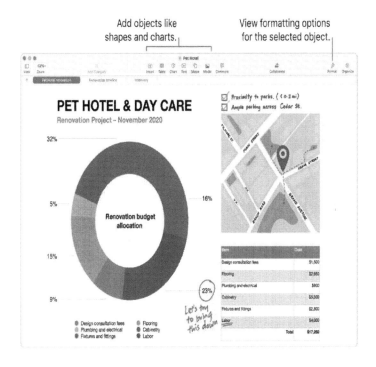

Work together using messages. You can invite people to work together in Messages, and everyone on the thread will be added to the Numbers spreadsheet instantly. Make sure Collaborate is chosen before selecting Messages after clicking the Share icon in the navigation bar. Choose the group's name if you want to include them as participants.

Cooperate in real time. With Activity Stream, you may view updates and remarks made by coworkers on a Numbers spreadsheet in a thorough list in the sidebar. Each modification, as well as who has been added to the spreadsheet or what file management updates have taken place, is simple to follow.

Organize your space with sheets. Use several sheets or tabs to display various informational viewpoints. Use one sheet for your budget, one for a table, and one for notes, for instance. To add a new sheet, click. To reorganize sheets, drag a tab left or right.

Click + to add a new sheet.　　Drag a tab left or right to reorder sheets.

View　Zoom 50%⌄ 　Add Category

+ 　Pet Hotel renovation　Renovation timeline　Inventory

Formulas are easy to use. Get built-in assistance for more than 250 potent functions by entering the equal sign (=) in a cell to display a sidebar listing of all the functions and their descriptions. Enter a formula to instantly receive suggestions.

Advice: Choose the range of cells containing the values to instantly calculate a set of values. You may see the total, average, minimum, maximum, and count of the selected data at the bottom of the window. To view even more options, click the Menu button in the lower right corner.

Construct pivot tables. Use a pivot table to examine any amount of data, swiftly categorize and summarize results, and spot intriguing patterns and trends by using a table or range of cells in a spreadsheet as your source data. You can alter the source data's cell range, add and rearrange data in a pivot table, make a copyable snapshot of a pivot table for use in other apps, and more.

 **Pages**

Create gorgeous documents and books on your Mac using the Pages software. Open Microsoft Word documents, edit them, and keep track of your own and other people's modifications. It's now simpler than ever to work together on a Pages document and keep track of every change as it happens thanks to Activity Stream.

Good job! It is simple to get started on any project using Pages' professional, ready-to-use templates for books, newsletters, reports, résumés, and more.

Work together using messages. Everyone in the thread is automatically added to the Pages page when you give an invitation to contribute in Messages. Make sure Collaborate is chosen before selecting Messages after clicking the Share icon in the navigation bar. Choose the group's name if you want to include them as participants.

Cooperate in real time. With Activity Stream, you can view revisions and comments made by coworkers on a Pages document in a thorough list in the sidebar. Each modification, as well as who has been added to the Pages document or what file management updates have taken place, is simple to follow.

One location for all of your formatting tools . To open the Format inspector, click the Format button on the toolbar. The formatting options for the selected item in your document will then be displayed.

Wrap text around images. In a written document with an image, the text automatically wraps around the image. The Format sidebar allows you to precisely control the text wrapping.

Move a graphic into a text block...   **...and the text wraps around the graphic automatically.**

Become an editor. Create interactive books in EPUB format using Pages' built-in book templates. Text, pictures, and even a table of contents can be added. When you're ready, you can publish your book in Apple

Books and make it accessible for download or purchase.

Begin on your Mac and end on your iPad. By logging in with the same Apple ID on all of your devices, you can keep your papers current so that you may start writing on one device and continue where you left off on another.

Translate quickly. Choose the text you wish to translate, Control-click it, then select Translate before selecting a language. You can download languages so you can work offline by going to the Language & Region settings in System Settings and clicking the Translation Languages option at the bottom. To translate text you've input, select "Replace with Translation." Not every language is offered.

To observe the changes you and other users make to a document, enable change tracking. The adjustments and comments made by each participant are color-coded, allowing you to identify who made each change. To see the change tracking toolbar, choose Edit > Track Changes.

 **Photos**

To manage, edit, and share your photographs and videos, as well as to keep your photo library current across all of your devices, use photographs and iCloud Photos. Your best photos are shown in photos, and it's simple to find and enjoy your favorites thanks to more robust search features. You can edit your photographs and movies like an expert with simple tools. And now that iCloud Shared Photo Library is available, you may share an album with up to five other people, who can all edit, organize, and add photos and videos.

Automatically create a personalized video of special moments.

View your photos by Years, Months, Days, or All Photos.

All of your devices' photo collections. When you use your iPhone to snap a photo, it instantly shows on all of your devices when you sign in with the same Apple ID. With iCloud photographs, you can browse, search, and share all the photographs and videos from all of your devices that are signed in with the same Apple ID. Additionally, any photo modifications you make show up on all of your devices. Open System Settings, select your Apple ID from the sidebar, select iCloud, and then turn on Photos to get started.

Configure the iCloud Shared Photo Library. To give the entire family more full memories, share images and movies in a separate repository. In the Photos app, shared library content smoothly coexists with your private content. A photo or video is added to the Shared Library, or it is edited, and the changes are made visible to everyone who has access to the library. One shared library that you and up to five other people can use is available to you.

You must be logged in with your Apple ID and have iCloud Photos enabled in order to configure iCloud Shared Photo Library. Select the Shared Library option, then click Get Started under Photos > Settings. You have the option of adding participants right away or at a later time. Choose whether to upload all of your old photographs and videos, photos and videos with specific individuals, photos and videos taken after a certain date, or manually pick photos and videos to add to the shared library. You can switch between seeing your Personal Library, the Shared Library, or both libraries at once in Photos when the Shared Library has been configured.

Your Shared Library can now contain images and videos. To use suggestions for photos or videos you might want to add, go to Photos > Settings, click the

Shared Library tab, then check Shared Library Suggestions and choose "Add People" to receive suggestions of photos or videos with specific people. To move individual photos or videos to your Shared Library, Control-click the photo or video in your Personal Library and choose "Move to Shared Library."

See suggestions for your Shared Library.

Choose to view Personal Library, Shared Library, or Both Libraries.

Shared to You. Photos that contacts in your Contacts send you via Messages will instantly show up in the Shared with You section of your Photos app. Your library contains pictures of things you're most likely to care about, including occasions you went to. You can open Messages and carry on the conversation by clicking the message bubble on a photo while browsing the images in the Photos app.

Edit with skill. With robust yet simple editing tools, produce distinctive images and films. To quickly alter a photo or video, use the editing tools above the image. Click Edit to get more potent editing options, then use Smart Sliders to produce polished results. Both photographs and movies can be cropped, rotated, exposed more, and added filters.

Engage with the text. On your computer and the internet, Live Text is able to recognize text in photos. On a Mac, you may copy text from a photo and paste it into any document. You can even click an image to contact a number or open a website. Select the text, Control-click it, and then select Translate to translate it. Not every language is offered.

Relive memorable occasions. Important events like birthdays, anniversaries, and vacations are captured in photos. The Live Photos and films in your photo collection come to life as you scroll. To have Photos generate a memorable movie with music, titles, moods, and transitions that you can edit and share, click Memories in the sidebar. All of your other iCloud Photos-enabled devices have access to your Memories.

Find the thing you're seeking. Photos hides duplicates, receipts, and screenshots while showcasing the best photos in your library. To view images by year, month, or day, use the buttons at the top of the images window. You can also select All Photos to view your whole collection in a flash. In order to search your images based on what's in them, the date they were taken, individuals you've identified in them, people you've attached captions to, and their location—if provided—images detects objects, scenes, and people in your photos and videos. Spotlight and Siri can both be used to look up images.

Dial Siri. Say something like, "Show me photos of Ursula."

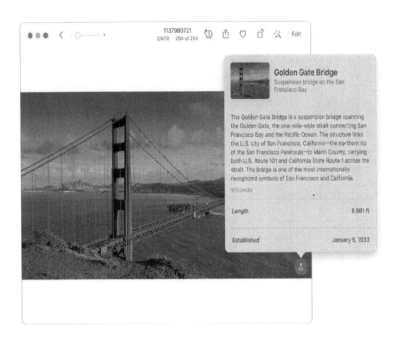

Golden Gate Bridge
Suspension bridge on the San Francisco Bay

The Golden Gate Bridge is a suspension bridge spanning the Golden Gate, the one-mile-wide strait connecting San Francisco Bay and the Pacific Ocean. The structure links the U.S. city of San Francisco, California—the northern tip of the San Francisco Peninsula—to Marin County, carrying both U.S. Route 101 and California State Route 1 across the strait. The bridge is one of the most internationally recognized symbols of San Francisco and California.

Wikipedia

Length	8,981 ft
Established	January 5, 1933

Things, places, and people. In your images, Visual Lookup can identify a lot of objects. To highlight recognizable subjects and settings, swipe up on a picture or click the information icon. Find out more about well-known works of art, famous places, novels, and many kinds of pet breeds. Click the Favorites icon ♡ that appears on their photo to make sure that images of individuals who are important to you are always at the top of the individuals album. To view all of your images with location information on an interactive map, use the Places album. To view more images from a certain place, zoom in on the map.

Tip: Any photo can have a location tagged on it. Click the Information button  while looking at the picture, then select Assign a Location and begin typing. Select a location from the drop-down menu, or type the address and hit Return.

Make up your own Live Photos. Use the Loop effect on Live Photos to repeatedly repeat the action, or Bounce to play the animation forward and backward. Use Long Exposure to blur motion in your Live Photos for a professional DSLR look. This will transform a common waterfall or running stream into a work of art.

**Podcasts**

To browse, subscribe to, and listen to your favorite podcasts on your Mac, use Apple Podcasts. Discovering new podcasts organized by topics you're interested in is made easier by personal recommendations.

Start by pressing "Listen Now." View all of the latest episodes for the podcasts you subscribe to in one location, along with personalized suggestions for podcasts you might enjoy. Any podcasts you're still listening to while logged in with your Apple ID are preserved in Listen Now, even if you started them on a different device.

Dial Siri. Say something like, "Play the previous podcast again," or "Keep listening to this podcast."

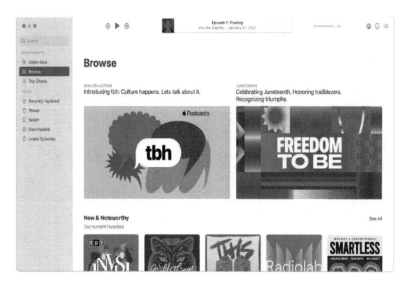

Find fresh podcasts. Find topic- and show-based podcast suggestions in Listen Now, or check out the hottest shows in Top Charts. If you find a show you enjoy, you can download an episode or subscribe to the podcast. In Shared with You, you can view the recommendations your friends make as well as receive recommendations for comparable topics and shows based on what you appreciate.

Presented to You. The episodes of podcasts that friends in your Contacts send you in Messages instantly show up in the new Shared with You section of Listen Now in Apple Podcasts.

Episodes can be saved to a library. Click to add a single episode to your library. Click ✛ Subscribe to receive notifications of new episodes for the whole podcast. Click ☁⬇ to download a podcast for later listening.

Lookup by host or visitor. Search results for a particular subject or person may include shows they host, shows on which they appear as guests, and even shows in which they are mentioned or discussed.

Follow the people you like. To make a show a favorite of yours and ensure that you never miss an episode, click Follow. Check out the Recently Updated area of your library to see what's fresh.

Use Quick Note to save ideas. Want to keep in mind a podcast to listen to on your next road trip or while exercising? Simply store the data to a Quick Note so you can locate it quickly in the future. Press Fn-Q or a designated Hot Corner in Podcasts to open Quick Note and save the podcast URL. The Quick Note can be found in the Notes app's sidebar later.

To play music, radio, or a podcast through an external speaker, utilize AirPlay. Screen Mirroring can be accessed by clicking the Control Center icon in the menu bar, then choosing an available speaker.

 **Preview**

Use the Preview app to view and edit PDFs and photos, complete and sign online forms, annotate PDFs, change the format of graphic files, batch edit files, password-protect PDFs, highlight and translate text, and much more.

Activate the PDF form. Click a form field in Preview, then enter your text. To save the form and continue filling it out later, select File > Export.

Put a password on a PDF file. Give a PDF a password that users must input in order to view the contents in order to safeguard it. Open the PDF file you wish to protect with a password in Preview, go to File > Export, and then choose Permissions. Choose Permissions, then enter an Owner Password password. Type it again to make sure, then click Apply and Save.

Tip: To produce a copy of the password-secured PDF while keeping the original PDF unencrypted, enter a new name for the PDF before saving.

You can add and remove PDF pages. Add, remove, or reorder pages in a PDF after opening it in Preview:

- Insert a new page after the current page by selecting the page you want to appear before it, selecting Edit > Insert, and then selecting "Page from File" or "Blank Page."
- To delete a page, pick the page or pages you wish to remove from the document by selecting View > Thumbnails or View > Contact Sheet, then click the Delete key on your keyboard (or select Edit > Delete).
- Drag pages to their new location by selecting View > Thumbnails or View > Contact Sheet.
- Drag thumbnail images from one PDF to the other to copy a page between them. To do this, select View > Thumbnails or View > Contact Sheet in each PDF.

Translate quickly. Choose the text you wish to translate, Control-click it, then select Translate before selecting a language. Go to the Language & Region settings under System Settings, then click the Translation Languages button at the bottom. You may also download languages so you can operate offline. Not every language is offered.

Observe and transform picture files. Images can be converted by Preview into a variety of file kinds, such as JPEG, JPEG 2000, PDF, PNG, PSD, TIFF, and more. Select File > Export, click the Format option, select a file type, enter a new name, and select a location for the file before clicking Save while the image is open in Preview. If the option you're looking for isn't shown in the Format menu, click the menu while holding down the Option key to explore more specific or vintage formats.

A tip: To convert many image files at once, open each one in a separate window, choose them from the window's sidebar (press Command-A to pick all), and then proceed as directed above. By selecting every picture file and selecting Tools > Adjust Size, you may easily batch resize image files.

 **Reminders**

Keeping track of all of your to-dos is now simpler than ever thanks to Reminders. Make reminders for shopping lists, job projects, or anything else you want to remember. Save Reminders lists as templates to reuse them in the future and utilize configurable features like Tags and Custom Smart Lists to organize your reminders to match your workflow. To collaborate and work together, you may also share a list with other people.

Insert tags. To arrange your reminders, add tags. In the sidebar, select one or more tags to easily filter reminders.

Make your own smart lists. Your forthcoming reminders are automatically sorted in Smart Lists according to dates, times, tags, places, flags, or priorities. By clicking Add List, choosing "Make into Smart List," and adding filters, you can create custom smart lists.

Lists can be saved as templates when they are made so that they can be used again and again. Choose File > Save as Template, then select the list in the sidebar.

View the upcoming events. Items are organized by time and date in the Today and Scheduled lists in the sidebar. Make sure to stay on top of forthcoming reminders so you don't miss a beat.

Make wise recommendations. Based on prior reminders you've generated, Reminders automatically proposes dates, times, and locations for a reminder.

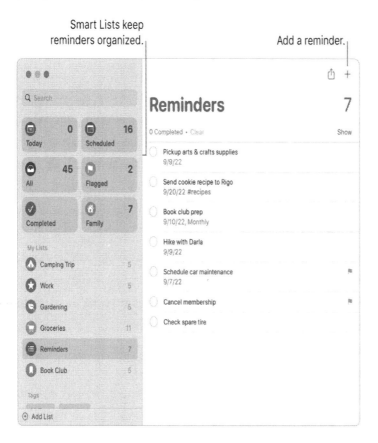

Work together on a list. In Mail or Messages, you can share the link or invite people to work together on a list. Select 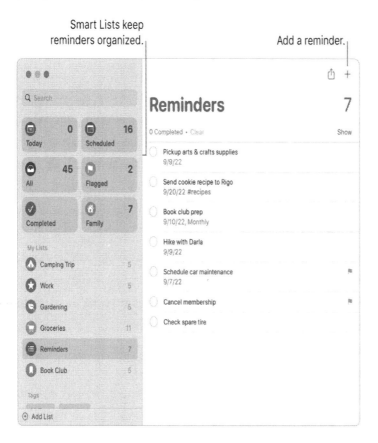 Messages, Mail, or Invite with Link after clicking . Everyone in the thread is automatically added to the list when you share in Messages. You can manage collaboration and keep track of activities once you've asked people to join.

Affirm accountability. People you share lists with can be given reminders so they get an alert. Make sure everyone is aware of their responsibilities by dividing up the work. Click in the menu bar and select how to share to distribute a list.

Use groups and subtasks to organize. Press Command-] or drag a reminder onto another one to make it a subtask. The subtask is indented beneath the parent reminder, which is made bold. To keep your view clear, you can collapse or expand your subtasks.

Select File > New Group to organize your reminders into groups. You can give the group any name you like. Drag other listings into the group to add them or drag them out to remove them.

View your accomplishments. The Completed Smart List in your sidebar allows you to view all of your completed reminders, along with the date that you checked each one off.

In Mail, get suggestions for reminders. Siri can identify potential reminders while you're communicating with someone in Mail and offer suggestions for how to set them up.

Quickly add a reminder. Use everyday words to make a reminder fast. Write "Take Amy to soccer every Wednesday at 5PM" for instance to set a recurring reminder for that time and day.

Dial Siri. Make a statement along the lines of, "Remind me to stop at the grocery store when I leave here."

 Safari

Users prefer Safari because of its speed, energy efficiency, and cutting-edge privacy features like passkeys. As long as you log into iCloud with the same Apple ID, you can use the same Safari on Mac, iPhone, and iPad thanks to the tab bar, extensions, and start page.

Start looking. Start typing a word or website URL, and Safari will display matching and recommended websites. Or pick an item from your Safari start page that you usually use or like. When a site is already open, you can start a new search by entering your search terms in the active tab.

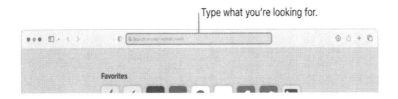

Type what you're looking for.

Customize your Safari start page. Favorites, reading list items, a privacy report, and more may appear on your start page. To use as a background image, you can import your own photo or pick from the available options. Additionally, you may sync your start page between devices. Click ⚙ in the bottom right corner of the start page to set the start page's parameters.

View several websites in a single window. To launch a new tab and type an address, click ✛ at the far right of the tab bar or press Command-T on your keyboard. As the size of the window changes, the tabs automatically resize.

Hold the pointer over a tab to
see a preview of the webpage.

Quickly view tab contents. You may quickly recognize a webpage by looking at its favicon, an emblem or logo linked with the website. To obtain a preview of the webpage's contents, hover the pointer over a tab.

Check out the sidebar. You can manage your tab groups, bookmarks, reading list, and shared with you links in the sidebar by clicking ⌄ the Sidebar button ▣. By clicking the arrow next to Tab Groups in the sidebar, you can also expand your tab groups to see all of your open tabs inside a group.

Utilize Tab Groups to organize. When conducting research for a task or trip, you can open multiple tabs, save them, and group them together. To create a group from the open tabs, click the Add Tab Group icon ⊞ while the sidebar is visible and then select New Tab Group. Alternately, select New Empty Tab Group and look for tabs to include in a Tab Group. The saved Tab Groups are present on the sidebar. Use the sidebar or the pop-up menu ⌄ to switch between Tab Groups if the sidebar is hidden.

Share ideas on Tab Groups. In Messages, you can invite others to work together on a Tab Group, and once you do, they are all added automatically. To share a tab group, click the button ⦁⦁⦁ next to it in the sidebar, select Share Tab Group, and then select Messages. Once you've shared a Tab Group, team members can add their own tabs, and when you're in the Tab Group, you can see what page other members are currently viewing.

You can view your tabs from any device that is logged into iCloud with the same Apple ID because Tab Groups are accessible across all of those devices.

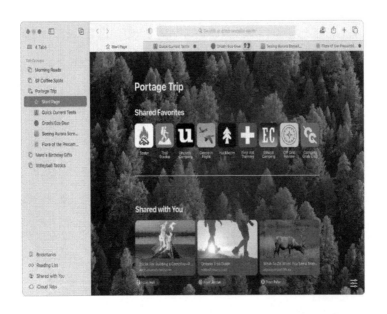

Use Focus to filter your web browsing. To organize your browsing, assign a certain Focus to Tab Groups. For instance, keep tabs that you use for work separate from ones that you use frequently. Select Focus from the sidebar by selecting Apple Menu > System Settings. On the right, select a Focus, such as Work, click ❯, and select Add Filter from the Focus Filters menu.

Passkeys can be used to secure your data. Passkeys let you login in to websites without sharing your password and instead utilize Touch ID or Face ID. Passkeys also function on non-Apple devices. Passkeys are stored in your iCloud keychain and are much more secure than two-factor authentication because they protect you against phishing and data leaks.

You must have Password & Keychain enabled in iCloud Settings in order to use passkeys. Choose to save a passkey for that website when you sign in. Use Touch ID or your iPhone or iPad to log in.

Presented to You. The Shared with You feature of the Safari start page and sidebar automatically displays interesting articles, recipes, and other links that friends in your Contacts share with you in Messages. You may read the stories you find in Safari and News wherever it's most convenient for you because they appear in both apps' sidebars.

Learn about extensions. Extensions give Safari extra features that let you customize your browsing. There are extensions that allow you to rapidly store material from your favorite websites, get coupons, correct your grammar, and block adverts. To access the extensions category in the App Store, select Safari > Safari Extensions. This will provide highlighted Safari extensions and categories (such as Browse Better, Read with Ease, Top Free Apps, etc.). Once you have them, enable them in Safari's settings. To enable extensions, choose the Extensions tab and then select the appropriate boxes.

Jot down notes on a website. With Quick Note, you may highlight and annotate immediately on a website, saving your notes for the next time you visit. Select

Add Quick Note by clicking the website's share icon⬆️
. Return to the webpage and press the thumbnail of the saved note to open it. Alternatively, open and see stored quick notes from the Notes sidebar.

Browse the internet anonymously and securely. When you visit a website that isn't secure or that might be attempting to deceive you into sharing your personal information, Safari automatically converts the site to HTTPS and alerts you to the possibility. It additionally defends you against cross-site tracking by locating and deleting the information that trackers leave behind. Before allowing a social network to view what you're doing on unaffiliated websites, Safari will request your consent. Additionally, Safari protects you from web monitoring by making it more difficult to identify your Mac. Utilizing your IP address to create a profile of you is prohibited by intelligent tracking prevention.

Keep your email address private. You can generate as many random, one-of-a-kind email addresses as you need with an iCloud+ membership, and you can do this whenever you need one (for instance, to fill out a form on a website). Any email sent to a Hide My Email address you create for a website is sent to your personal email account. Hide My Email addresses allow you to receive email without disclosing your actual email address, and you can disable one at any moment.

Check out a privacy report. To view the cross-site trackers that Safari is blocking on each website, click

(i) the Privacy Report button 🛡 to the left of the active tab. This will help you better understand how a site treats your privacy. To view a privacy report with more information on the website's active trackers, go here.

Website translation. In Safari, you can rapidly translate whole websites. The website address box in Safari displays a translate button 🔤 when you land on a page that it can translate. To switch between languages, click. To indicate when a webpage has been translated, the button's color 🔤 changes.

Note that not all languages or regions support translation features. A list of the languages that are offered may be seen at Safari: Web Page Translation.

Tip: Force-click a word on a webpage to view its definition or, if there is one available, a Wikipedia article. To find out more, try forcing clicking text in other applications like Messages or Mail.

 **Shortcuts**

With just one click or by using Siri, you can do multi-step tasks quickly using the Shortcuts app. Make shortcuts to move text from one program to another, receive instructions to the next event on your calendar, and more. To execute many steps in a task, use pre-made shortcuts from the Shortcuts Gallery or create your own using various tools.

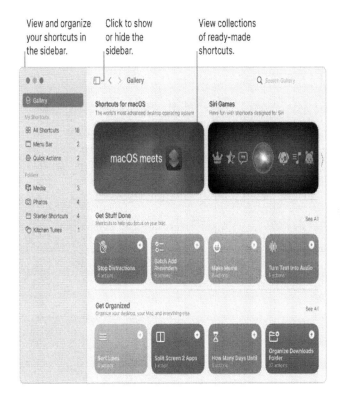

A range of potential outcomes. In the Gallery, browse or perform a search for shortcuts. A variety of typical tasks are accessible with starter shortcuts that are compiled into collections. Your customized shortcuts, along with any pre-made shortcuts you select or modify, are displayed in My Shortcuts in the Gallery sidebar. By clicking the Sidebar button , the Gallery sidebar can be displayed or hidden.

Create your own shortcuts. To get the outcome you want, create a new shortcut and then drag activities from the list on the right to the shortcut editor on the left. Similar to how steps in a task constitute the foundation of a shortcut, actions are. Choose from a variety of options, like copying the current URL from Safari, creating a folder, or retrieving the most recent photo from the Photos app. Additionally, you can employ script-running operations like rounding numbers, activating airplane mode, and performing calculations. Additionally, Shortcuts offers "next action" recommendations to assist you in finishing your shortcut.

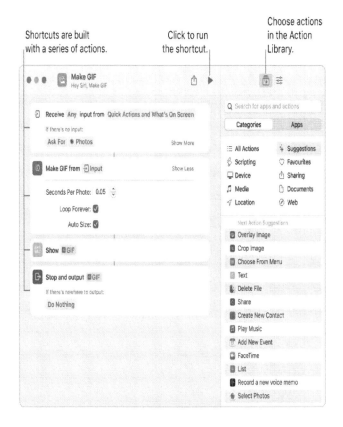

Shortcuts are built with a series of actions.

Click to run the shortcut.

Choose actions in the Action Library.

Your own personal shortcuts. The easiest approach to complete a task is to use Siri to perform a shortcut. Additionally, you can add shortcuts to the Services menu of programs, the menu bar, and the Dock. When you double-click a shortcut, you can select choices under Use as Quick Action by clicking Shortcut Details.

Dial Siri. something along the lines of "Text last image."

Share and sync shortcuts. Your shortcuts will appear on all of your devices when you sign in using the same Apple ID. Your other devices automatically update when you make changes on one of them. You can both provide and receive shared shortcuts. You can share your shortcuts with others. To share, double-click the shortcut, click, and then select the sharing method. To the Share Sheet in the sidebar, you can now add shortcuts for frequently performed operations.

 **Stocks**

The Stocks app is the best tool for Mac market tracking. View prices in the personalized watchlist, click a stock to view more information and an interactive chart, and read stories from Apple News to learn more about the market trends.

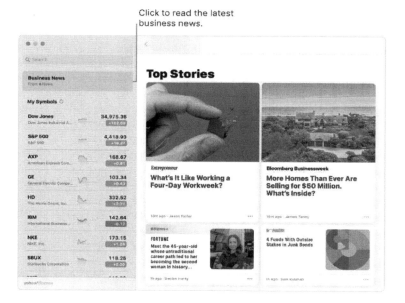

Click to read the latest business news.

The United States, Canada, the United Kingdom, and Australia all offer access to Apple News stories and Top Stories. Yahoo offers news items from numerous nations and regions.

Make your watchlists unique by creating them. Click My Symbols, followed by New Watchlist, to add a watchlist. Enter a company name or stock symbol in the Search form to add a stock to your watchlist. To view stock information, double-click the stock symbol in the search results. Click ✛ the in the top-right corner, select the watchlist you want the stock to be added to, and then click to add it. Control-click the stock symbol and select "Manage Symbol" to remove a stock. Then, deselect the checkbox next to the stock in the watchlist you want to remove it from. A stock on your watchlist can also be opened in a new tab or window by controlling-clicking it.

Verify market alterations. When viewing your watchlist, toggle between price change, percentage change, and market capitalization by clicking the green or red button next to each price. Color-coded sparklines that track performance throughout the day are also included in the watchlist.

Read articles on the businesses you are interested in. Click a stock in your watchlist to get an interactive chart, more information, and the most recent corporate news. To view a selection of current business stories, click Business News at the top of the watchlist.

Click to cycle between price change, percentage change, and market capitalization.

Take a closer look. Want to see how the market performed the previous week, month, or year? To view prices in the timeframe you want most, use the icons above the chart.

on each of your devices, your watchlist. When you check in with the same Apple ID on all of your devices, your watchlist will remain consistent.

Advice: On your Mac, open the Stocks widget in Notification Center for a fast glance at the current market.

TV

Use the Apple TV app to watch all of your movies and TV shows. Purchase or rent movies and TV shows, join a channel subscription plan, and resume where you left off on any of your devices.

Start watching now to get going. Browse a carefully selected feed of suggestions in Watch Now based on the movies and TV shows you've seen or the channels you've subscribed to.

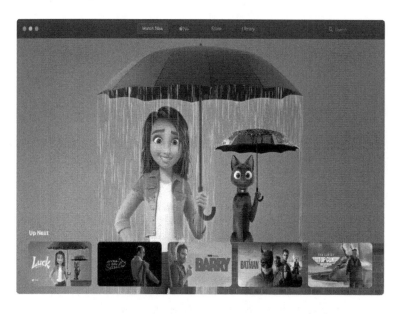

Utilize the Apple TV app to watch Luck

Watch Up Next indefinitely. You can see the movies and TV shows you've added to your queue as well as the ones you're currently watching in Up Next. Click the Add to Up Next button to add a new movie or TV show.

Learn more about Kids, TV Shows, and Movies. Click the Movies, TV Shows, or Kids tab in the navigation bar and then explore by genre if you're looking for something specific.

Purchase, rent, or join. You have the option to buy or rent a movie or TV show when you find one you wish to watch. All devices can access the channels you've subscribed to, and through Family Sharing, up to six family members can use them.

View the sharing of your friends. You can view shows and movies that your friends and family share with you using the Messages app whenever it suits you. Simply seek for them in the Watch Now part of the Shared With You portion of the Apple TV app. Only anything that was sent by someone you have in your Contacts will show up in Shared with You.

Watch Together. FaceTime allows you to connect with friends, and SharePlay allows you to watch a movie or TV show with them while exchanging comments in Messages. Move the mouse pointer over any item in the TV app, then press the Play button to begin watching. You may use your iPhone to talk with pals while watching material on your Mac. Additionally, audio is automatically adjusted with smart volume so that you can communicate even in loud environments.

Note: To utilize SharePlay, your Mac must be running macOS version 12.3 or later, and your iPad must be running iPadOS 15.4 or more. Some SharePlay-compatible apps demand a membership in order to function. Not every country or location has access to every feature and piece of information.

Select a book from your personal collection. To view all of the movies and TV series you've bought or downloaded, arranged by genre, click Library. Just click the movie or TV show to begin viewing.

 **Voice Notes**

Recording private reminders, classroom lectures, interviews, or even song ideas is now simpler than ever thanks to Voice Memos. You may listen to the voice memos you record on your iPhone directly on your MacBook Air thanks to iCloud.

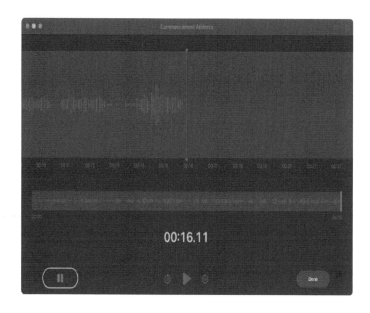

Using your MacBook Air, record. To begin recording, click the Record button . To stop, click Done. A recording's name can be changed to make it simpler to locate. After selecting the default name, type a new one. Click the Play button ▶ to start listening to your recording.

Across all of your devices, your voice memos. When you login in with the same Apple ID across all of your devices, you may access recordings you made on your iPhone or iPad directly from your Mac.

Use folders to organize. To keep your voice memos organized, use folders. Click the Sidebar button ⬜, then at the bottom of the sidebar, click the New Folder button to add a folder. Click Save after giving the folder a name. Press and hold the Option key while you drag a recording into the folder to add it to the folder.

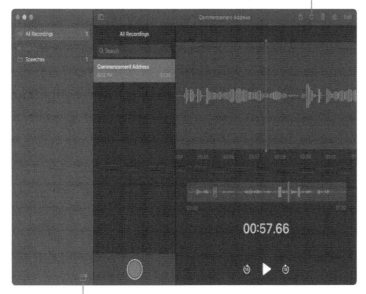

Create new folders to
organize your recordings.

Add a record to your favorites. To conveniently locate a recording later, select it, then click the Favorite button ♡ in the toolbar. The Sidebar button ⊞ will display all of your favorites.

Don't be silent. Skip over any audio pauses. Toggle Skip Silence on by clicking the Playback Settings icon at the top of the Voice Memos window.

The playback speed can be altered. You can alter the speed of your audio. Drag the slider left or right after clicking the Playback Settings icon at the top of the Voice Memos window.

Make a recording better. Reduce background noise and room reverberation to improve the sound quality of your voice memos. Turn on Enhance Recording by selecting the Playback Settings button at the top of the Voice Memos window.

Chapter 4

Use the macOS User Guide

There is a lot more information on using your MacBook Air in the macOS User Guide.

Get support. To launch the macOS User Guide, click the Finder icon in the Dock, then select macOS Help from the Help option in the menu bar. Alternately, enter a query or keyword in the search bar and select a subject from the list of results.

Show the table of contents.

Learn about macOS.

Discover subjects. You can browse or search the macOS User Guide to discover a topic. pick "Table of Contents" to view the themes, then pick a topic to read it, to navigate. Or, to get to your solution straight away, type what you're looking for into the search box.

Click > to view more topics.

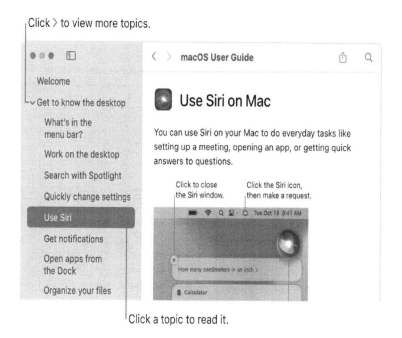

Click a topic to read it.

Discover what is new. To learn more about the newest features of macOS, select "See What's New in macOS" from the Help menu.

Search for a menu item in Help if you can't recall where it is in an app. When you hover the pointer over the outcome, an arrow pointing to the command appears.

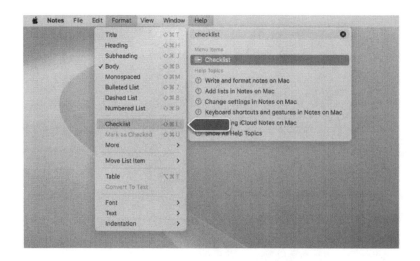

Are you a new Mac user?

Here are some tips to help you get started if this is your first Mac computer, especially if you came from a Windows environment.

Learn how to use the computer's desktop. You perform your job on the desktop, where you may open applications fast, perform searches, and organize files.

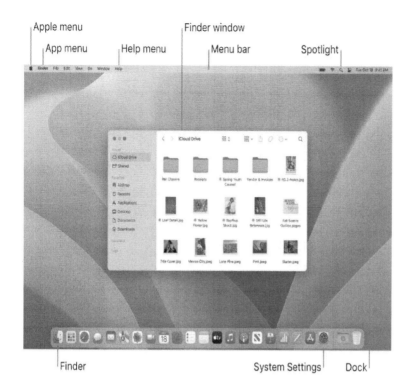

Apple menu

App menu   Help menu   Finder window

Menu bar   Spotlight

Finder   System Settings   Dock

On the desktop you'll find:

- **The menu bar** is always located at the top of the screen, whether it is for the desktop or the currently open app. To access options and do activities in apps, use the menus.

- **The Dock:** Located at the bottom of the desktop, the Dock resembles Windows' taskbar and Start menu but may be moved using System Settings. The Dock makes it simple to see every open program and swiftly launch your preferred apps.

Click an app's icon in the Dock to launch it. Launchpad also allows you to launch apps.

- **The Finder:** Click 🔍 in the Dock to launch the Finder, which is comparable to Windows' File Explorer in how you may organize and find your files. To choose between icons ⊞, a list ☰, columns ⦀, or a gallery ▭ view of your files, use the buttons at the top of the Finder window. When a file is selected in any view, pressing the Space bar will display a Quick Look preview without opening the selected file.

- **The Spotlight menu:** With Spotlight, you can search through any file or contact on your Mac, including emails, documents, and more. Additionally, you may open apps and conduct web searches. Click the Spotlight symbol 🔍 in the top right corner of the screen or press Command-Space to launch Spotlight.

- **System Settings:** System Settings ⚙ is comparable to Windows' Control Panel. Setup options for the desktop, Dock, display, Bluetooth, network, and a lot more allow you to personalize your Mac.

Learn how to use the trackpad and keyboard.

Generally speaking, the Mac's Command key⌘ and Windows' Control key are the same. Use Command-C and Command-V, for instance, to copy and paste material. On a Mac, the Return key corresponds to the Windows Enter key, whereas the Delete key corresponds to the Backspace key. Press Fn-Delete to forward a deleted message.

Use the trackpad to quickly scroll, swipe, right-click, force-click, click, and resize documents.

Add applications. Apps can be downloaded online or from the App Store. You receive a package file (.pkg) or disk image file (.dmg) when you download a software from the internet. Locate the.dmg or.pkg file for the app in your Downloads folder, double-click it, and then adhere to the on-screen directions to complete the installation. After installing the app, you are prompted to remove the disk image or package file.

Find the app in the Applications folder in Finder and drag it to the Trash to uninstall it. Some apps come with an uninstaller that you can use to remove the software and any related files.

Close, maximize, and minimize windows. A single app can have numerous windows open at once. To resize and close windows, use the buttons in the top-left corner of the window.

- To close the window but not the app, click the Close Window button or press Command-W. To close all of the application's open windows, press Option-Command-W. To close the application, press Command-Q.

- To minimize a window, click the Minimize Window button (or press Command-M). When a window is minimized, the app remains open, but the window is reduced to an icon on the right side of the Dock. To return the window to its original size, click the icon.

- To launch your app in full-screen mode, click the Full-Screen Window button . Holding down the Option key while clicking the button will maximize the window. To see further options, including tiling the window, you may also mouse over the button. To restore the window to its original size, press Esc.

Adjust windows. To reposition a window, drag it by the title bar. Some windows are immovable.

Open different app windows. To rapidly go back to the previous app, use Command-Tab. To display icons for all open apps when you have numerous app windows open, hold Command while pressing Tab. Press Tab (or the arrow keys) to switch between the apps while holding Command, then choose the one you wish to be active. To operate in the open app, release the Command key.

Generate a screenshot. The Screenshot Utility can be used by pressing Command-Shift-5.

Give Siri jobs to complete. Click the Siri symbol in the top right corner of the screen to launch Siri. You can either say "Hey Siri" (if the option is enabled) or hit the Dictation/Siri key (F5), pressing and holding Command-Space bar. Ask Siri to do things like open a folder, open an app, brighten the screen, and more.

Use the Apple Watch, iPad, and iPhone with your Mac. You can effortlessly exchange files and photographs, edit papers, take calls, answer emails, and send text messages between devices if you sign in to all of your Apple devices with the same Apple ID.

Keyboard shortcuts on your Mac

On your MacBook Air, you can use key combinations to do actions that you would typically perform with a trackpad, mouse, or other device. These are some of the most used keyboard shortcuts.

Note: Depending on the language and keyboard layout you're using on your Mac, keyboard shortcuts in programs may change. If any of the shortcuts below don't function as you would expect, check the app menus in the menu bar to find the right ones. The keyboard viewer can also be used to observe your current keyboard layout, sometimes referred to as an input source.

Shortcut	Description
Command-X	Cut the selected item and copy it to the Clipboard.
Command-C	Copy the selected item to the Clipboard.
Command-V	Paste the contents of the Clipboard into the current document or app.
Command-Z	Undo the previous command. Press Command-Shift-Z to redo.
Command-A	Select all items.
Command-F	Open a Find window, or find items in a document.
Command-G	Find the next occurrence of the item you're searching for. Press Command-Shift-G to find the previous occurrence.
Command-H	Hide the windows of the front app. Press Command-Option-H to view the front app but hide all other apps.
Command-M	Minimize the front window to the Dock. Press Command-Option-M to minimize all windows of the front app.
Command-N	Open a new document or window.
Command-O	Open the selected item, or open a dialog to select a file to open.
Command-P	Print the current document.
Command-S	Save the current document.
Command-W	Close the front window. Press Command-Option-W to close all windows of the app.
Command-Q	Quit the current app.

Security features for MacBook Air

The security protections on your MacBook Air with Apple silicon protect the data on your computer and stop illegal software apps from launching during startup. These features include:

- Secure startup: Support for secure startup is activated on automatically. It is made to make sure that the operating system software that loads when your machine first turns on is approved by Apple.

  If an untrusted component is what prevents your MacBook Air from starting, it boots up from a safe recovery partition and, if it can, fixes problems on its own.

- Secure storage: To provide high levels of security, your MacBook Air storage drive is encrypted with hardware keys. You must back up your files to an external source because data recovery may not be possible in the event of a catastrophic failure.

  To frequently backup your files, you can set up Time Machine or another backup strategy.

- System integrity: Your MacBook Air's Apple silicon is built to check that the version of macOS loaded during startup is permitted by Apple and works silently in the background to safeguard the authorizations set up for macOS. By doing this, dangerous software and websites have a harder time exploiting your Mac.
- Data Protection: Third-party app developers can employ file-level encryption to further safeguard sensitive data without affecting system performance in addition to the storage disk encryption that is enabled by default in MacBook Air.

Note: Your MacBook Air could become unresponsive under unusual situations, including a power outage during a macOS upgrade, and the chip's firmware might need to be revived.

Save space on your MacBook Air

By making files available only when needed, Optimize Storage allows you to automatically free up space on your MacBook Air. Your older files will be kept in iCloud and on the IMAP or Exchange server for your email so you may download them whenever you choose.

Additionally, there are tools for locating and erasing large files.

Improve storage. Go to Apple menu > System Settings, then choose General on the sidebar to get storage recommendations. To get several recommendations based on how your Mac is set up, click Storage on the right.

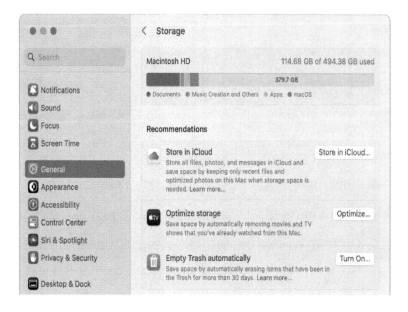

• Store in iCloud: Store all documents, images, and communications in iCloud to free up space on your Mac.

• Desktop and Documents: iCloud Drive may be used to store all of the files in your Desktop and

Documents folders. iCloud Drive keeps recently opened files on your Mac and makes your oldest files available when you require storage space.

- Messages: Keep all correspondence—including attachments—in iCloud. ICloud preserves recent attachments on your Mac and makes your oldest files available when you require storage space.

You can access your files on your MacBook Air exactly where you left them, despite the fact that they are saved on the cloud.

- Improve storage: Make the Apple TV app's storage of movies and TV shows as efficient as possible to free up space on your Mac. After watching a movie or a television show, you can select to have it instantly removed from your MacBook Air. You are always welcome to download them again.
- Automatic trash emptying: Delete trash things that have been there for longer than 30 days.
- Mac OS also:
- Prevents you from downloading the same file repeatedly from Safari

- Notifies you when you're ready to remove installer software after installing a new app.
- Removes safe logs and caches when you're running low on storage

Take a screenshot on your Mac

Find all the controls you require to take screenshots and screen recordings by exploring the Screenshot menu. During a screen recording, your voice can also be recorded. You can simply share, edit, and save screenshots and videos thanks to the workflow that has been improved.

Enter the controls for the screenshot. Command-Shift-5 is pressed. The entire screen, a particular window, or a section ⬚ of a window can be captured. Additionally, you have the option of recording the full screen ⬚ or a certain area of it.

To capture a selection, record your screen, and other functions, use the icons at the bottom of the screen. To change your save location, timer before capturing, microphone and audio parameters, or to display the pointer, click parameters. To take a screenshot or record a video, click Capture or Record.

A thumbnail shows up in the bottom right corner of the screen when you take a screenshot or video. To edit or share the thumbnail, click on it or swipe to the right to quickly save it in a document or folder.

Aside from going to the Apps > Utilities folder in the Finder or the Other folder in Launchpad, you may also access the Screenshot utility from those locations.

Mark the screenshot you took. To use Markup tools to annotate your snapshot, click the image. Right from the screenshot, click Share ⬆️to send your annotated screen to coworkers or friends.

Mac resources, service, and support

Additional information on your MacBook Air is available online, in Apple Diagnostics, System Report, and other places.

Computer Report. Use System Report to learn more about your MacBook Air. It displays information such as the operating system version, serial number, operating system, installed RAM, and installed hardware and applications. Select Apple menu > About This Mac, then click More Info to see System Report. Click System Report after that.

Diagnostics for Apple. If you're trying to figure out if the memory or CPU of the machine are malfunctioning, you can utilize Apple Diagnostics to aid. Apple Diagnostics assists in locating the probable cause of a hardware issue and offers initial actions to attempt and fix it. If you require additional assistance, Apple Diagnostics will also assist you in contacting AppleCare Support.

Disconnect any external hardware, such as a hard drive or external display, before using Apple

Diagnostics. Ensure that the MacBook Air has an internet connection.

Restart the computer, hold the power button down for 10 seconds to bring up Startup Options, then press Command-D to launch Apple Diagnostics on a MacBook Air.

Choose your location's language if requested. Click the right arrow button or use the Return key. It takes a few minutes to finish the fundamental Apple Diagnostics test. If a problem is discovered, a description of the problem and additional instructions displays. Before leaving Apple Diagnostics, make a note of any reference numbers in case you need to get in touch with AppleCare assistance.

Online sources. Visit Welcome to Apple Support for information on online service and support. You may access information about Apple devices, view online user manuals, check for software updates, connect with other Apple users, and contact Apple for service, support, and expert guidance.

AppleCare assistance. AppleCare agents can assist you with troubleshooting, installing, and opening apps if you need it. Dial the support center number that is most convenient for you (the first 90 days are free). When you contact, be prepared with the purchase date and your MacBook Air serial number.

On the internet, at Contact Apple for support and service, you may find a comprehensive list of support phone numbers. Local and long-distance calling costs can be applicable, and phone numbers are subject to change.

Your free 90-day phone support period starts on the day of purchase.

Made in the USA
Middletown, DE
28 February 2024

50514799R00149